WALKIN

CENTR

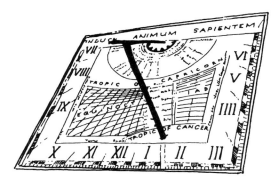

Paul Hannon

HILLSIDE

HILLSIDE GUIDES - ACROSS THE NORTH

Long Distance Walks
- COAST TO COAST WALK • CLEVELAND WAY COMPANION
- WESTMORLAND WAY • FURNESS WAY • CUMBERLAND WAY
- DALES WAY • LADY ANNE'S WAY • NORTH BOWLAND TRAVERSE

Circular Walks - Lancashire
- BOWLAND • PENDLE & THE RIBBLE

Circular Walks - Yorkshire Dales
- HOWGILL FELLS • THREE PEAKS • MALHAMDALE
- WHARFEDALE • NIDDERDALE • WENSLEYDALE • SWALEDALE

Circular Walks - North York Moors
- WESTERN MOORS • SOUTHERN MOORS • NORTHERN MOORS

Circular Walks - South Pennines
- BRONTE COUNTRY • CALDERDALE • ILKLEY MOOR

Circular Walks - Peak District
- EASTERN PEAK • NORTHERN PEAK • CENTRAL PEAK
- SOUTHERN PEAK • WESTERN PEAK

Circular Walks - North Pennines
- TEESDALE • EDEN VALLEY

Hillwalking - Lake District
- OVER LAKELAND MOUNTAINS • OVER LAKELAND FELLS

Yorkshire Pub Walks
- HARROGATE/WHARFE VALLEY • HAWORTH/AIRE VALLEY

Large format colour hardback

FREEDOM OF THE DALES

BIKING COUNTRY
- YORKSHIRE DALES CYCLE WAY • WEST YORKSHIRE CYCLE WAY
- MOUNTAIN BIKING - WEST & SOUTH YORKSHIRE
- AIRE VALLEY BIKING GUIDE • CALDERDALE BIKING GUIDE
- GLASGOW Clyde Valley & Loch Lomond

• YORK WALKS *City Theme Walks*

• WALKING COUNTRY TRIVIA QUIZ *Over 1000 questions*

Send S.A.E. for a detailed catalogue and pricelist

WALKING COUNTRY

CENTRAL PEAK

Paul Hannon

HILLSIDE

HILLSIDE
PUBLICATIONS
11 Nessfield Grove
Keighley
West Yorkshire
BD22 6NU

First published 1997

© Paul Hannon 1997

ISBN 1 870141 51 2

Whilst the author has walked and researched all the routes for the purposes of this guide, no responsibility can be accepted for any unforeseen circumstances encountered while following them. The publisher would, however, greatly appreciate any information regarding material changes, and any problems encountered.

The author would like to acknowledge the assistance of Roland Smith, Head of Information Services at the Peak National Park, for his invaluable help in looking over the manuscript. Any errors, however, remain the author's.

Cover illustrations: The Wye at Bakewell;
Hope Valley from Mam Tor; Abney Moor
Back cover: The stepping stones, Chee Dale
(Paul Hannon/Big Country Picture Library)

Page 1: Sundial, Eyam
Page 3: Ancient tombs, Bakewell

Printed in Great Britain by
Carnmor Print and Design
95-97 London Road
Preston
Lancashire
PR1 4BA

CONTENTS

INTRODUCTION

THE PEAK NATIONAL PARK

The Peak District was designated Britain's first National Park in 1951, and embracing an area of 555 square miles it is the most popular in the country. While commonly allotted to Derbyshire, substantial parts fall within Staffordshire, Yorkshire and Cheshire. *Peak* is in fact a misnomer, for it is plainly evident that peaks are in very short supply here: it derives from *Pecsaetan* ('hill-dweller'), tribes that occupied the area long before the Normans came.

The Peak divides into two distinctive areas, the Dark Peak and the White Peak. These refer to the principal rocks, millstone grit (gritstone) in the Dark Peak and limestone in the White Peak. The Dark Peak horseshoe encloses the limestone country, with the high moors of Kinder Scout and Bleaklow to the north and long arms reaching down either side. That in the east traces the Derwent Valley south in a series of abrupt edges: that to the west is disjointed, resurrecting itself above Buxton to run south, largely less dramatically, west of the Manifold Valley. The northern massif is typified by vast tracts of peat bog and heather, a world away from the White Peak's softer terrain.

The compact White Peak offers green dales overlooked by gleaming cliffs. Unlike the limestone country of the Yorkshire Dales, it has few potholes and pavements: its speciality is valleys, exemplified by the likes of Lathkill Dale, the river Wye and the incomparable Dovedale. Much of the White Peak is an upland plateau where old lead mining communities huddle. The area is dissected by drystone walls, and though large-scale quarrying is all too evident, farming remains the traditional source of employment, increasingly supplemented by tourism. While one railway survives to run through the heart of the Park, several others have been converted to leisure trails: they provide excellent cross-country routes linking numerous towns and villages.

Bakewell is the largest community in the National Park, but it is the small towns on the fringe, such as Buxton, Ashbourne, Matlock, Leek, Chapel en le Frith and Glossop, that act as major centres. Though this whole area might be encircled in a day's car tour, once you get out in the fresh air you will quickly appreciate the rich diversity of country that offers many happy years of real exploring - on foot.

CENTRAL PEAK

The Central Peak ranges from Mam Tor and Castleton in the north to the river Wye and Bakewell in the south. To the east the river Derwent, and Hathersage, form a natural boundary, while to the west the area tapers towards Buxton. Such is the compactness that surrounding areas crowd in on all sides: from the Mam Tor ridge we gaze upon Kinder Scout; across the Derwent are the celebrated Eastern gritstone edges; immediately south of Bakewell is delectable Lathkill Dale, and Buxton heralds the edge of Western Peakland.

Limestone and gritstone country, White and Dark Peak, meet here in the heart of the National Park, resulting in an unusually varied range of walks. Four take advantage of the colourful moorland in the Hathersage-Bradwell-Eyam triangle, while four more spring from the Hope Valley to sample Lose Hill and Win Hill on the fringes of the Vale of Edale. The area's main river, the Wye, is a springboard for numerous walks in captivating limestone scenery. From Chee Dale to Bakewell we sample the river's many facets, as it cuts through richly wooded, cliff-girt slopes in Miller's Dale, Water-cum-Jolly and Monsal Dale. A host of side valleys radiate, with Monk's Dale, Cressbrook Dale and Tideswell Dale at the forefront; Peter Dale, Hay Dale and a pair of Deep Dales represent the less frequented gems.

Shadowing the Wye, sometimes at a distance but often clinging like a limpet, is the Monsal Trail, a walkers' route created on a former railway line. Several of the walks incorporate sections, including some fascinating spells deep in the limestone gorge.

Besides Bakewell and Castleton, immensely popular villages include Tideswell, Eyam and Ashford in the Water. Additionally, Foolow, Great Longstone, Chelmorton and Great Hucklow feature among numerous other delightful villages. History abounds: Haddon Hall near Bakewell is a nationally renowned medieval manor house, while Bakewell itself merits a leisurely walk of discovery. An Iron Age hillfort occupies Fin Cop above Monsal Dale, in addition to the better known Mam Tor; while a fine Neolithic tomb is seen at Fivewells, near Chelmorton. Lead mining remains abound in the limestone uplands, while the caves of the Castleton area are justly famous.

This then, in a nutshell, is the Central Peak, the most compact, varied walking area you could wish for!

Access

Unlike the northern moors and eastern edges, which cover vast tracts of rolling moorland and are subject to numerous access agreements, the central and southern parts of the Peak can be accessed without problem using the extensive rights of way network. The small areas of truly open country that do exist already have good paths, so that the only times we resort to non rights of way are on odd occasions where concession paths have been negotiated or offered to open up popular areas, the best example in this book being the section of the Wye at Water-cum-Jolly. Additionally, the length of the Monsal Trail and link paths are used in similar vein.

Bakewell Bridge

Please take extra care to respect the life and work of the Peak. Its very accessibility puts it in the firing line when we all want to escape into the countryside at the same time. We can avoid creating undue work and expense for those custodians of the landscape, the farmers, by ensuring that dogs are kept on leads and that gates are closed after opening. If we take nothing more than photographs and leave only the slightest of footprints, then this wonderful landscape will still be in good shape for the next generation.

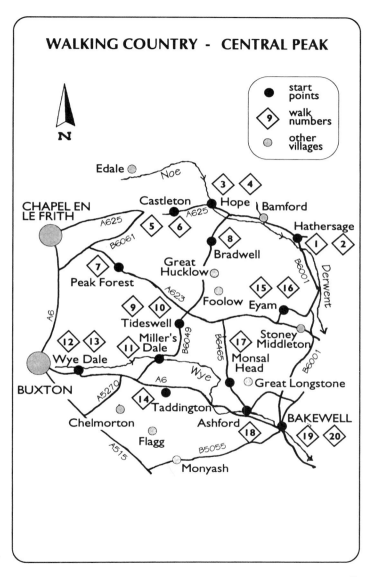

WALKING COUNTRY - CENTRAL PEAK

N

●	start points
◇9	walk numbers
●	other villages

Edale

Noe

CHAPEL EN LE FRITH

Castleton   Hope   Bamford

A625   A625

⟨3⟩ ⟨4⟩

Hathersage

⟨5⟩ ⟨6⟩

⟨1⟩ ⟨2⟩

B6061

⟨8⟩

Bradwell

B6001

⟨7⟩

Great Hucklow

Peak Forest

Derwent

A623

⟨15⟩ ⟨16⟩

Foolow   Eyam

⟨9⟩ ⟨10⟩

Tideswell

Stoney Middleton

⟨12⟩ ⟨13⟩

Miller's Dale

B6049

⟨17⟩

B6465

B6001

Wye Dale

⟨11⟩

Monsal Head

BUXTON

A5270

A6

Wye

Great Longstone

⟨14⟩

Taddington

Chelmorton

Ashford

BAKEWELL

Flagg

⟨18⟩

⟨19⟩ ⟨20⟩

A515

B5055

Monyash

9

Getting around

Without doubt Bakewell is focal point of the area, being well placed for access to all these walks. Though marginally outwith the scope of the walks, Buxton is equally well placed to the west. Bus services run between the two and radiate to many of the villages. The A6 links these towns and again provides an obvious jumping off point. The north and east of the area is well served by the Sheffield-Manchester (Hope Valley) railway, with stations at Grindleford, Hathersage, Bamford, Hope and Edale. The cul-de-sac line to Buxton is also useful.

Numerous seasonal bus services also operate on less regular routes. With a little planning, various permutations can be created by linking different sections of the walks, to create longer routes or to take advantage of public transport. Starting points with public transport, however limited, are indicated, along with other useful information, at the start of each walk.

Using the guide

Each walk is self-contained, with essential information being followed by a simple map and concise description of the route. Dovetailed between this are useful notes of features along the way, and interspersed are illustrations which both capture the flavour of the walks and record the many items of interest. In order to make the instructions easier to follow, essential route description has been highlighted in bold type, while items in lighter type refer to historical asides and things to look out for: in this format you can find your way more easily while still locating features of interest at the relevant point in the text.

The simple sketch maps identify the location of the routes rather than the fine detail, and whilst the route description should be sufficient to guide you around, an Ordnance Survey map is recommended: the route can easily be plotted on the relevant OS map. To gain the most from a walk, the detail of the 1:25,000 maps is unsurpassed. They also serve to vary walks as desired, giving an improved picture of one's surroundings and the availability of linking paths. Two maps give complete coverage of the walks:-
- *Outdoor Leisure Sheet 1 - Peak District, Dark Peak*
- *Outdoor Leisure Sheet 24 - Peak District, White Peak*

Also extremely useful for general planning purposes are the Landranger maps at 1:50,000, and again, two sheets cover the entire area:
110, Sheffield & Huddersfield; 119, Buxton, Matlock & Dove Dale
One further planning aid is the OS Touring Map which covers the whole National Park at the scale of 1:63,360 (1 inch to the mile).

SOME USEFUL ADDRESSES

Ramblers' Association   1/5 Wandsworth Road, London SW8 2XX
Tel. 0171-582 6878

Peak National Park Office
Aldern House, Baslow Road, Bakewell DE45 1AE
Tel. 01629-816200

Bakewell Visitor Centre   Tel. 01629-813227

Castleton Visitor Centre   Tel. 01433-620679
(weekends only in winter)

Edale Visitor Centre Tel. 01433-670207

Tourist Information
The Crescent **Buxton** Derbyshire SK17 6BQ
Tel. 01298-25106

Peak & Northern Footpaths Society
Mr E Sutton, 1 Crossfield Grove, Marple Bridge, Cheshire SK6 5EQ
Tel. 0161-427 3582

Friends of National Parks
Council for National Parks, 246 Lavender Hill, London SW11 1LJ
Tel. 071-924 4077

Derbyshire Wildlife Trust
Elvaston Castle, Derby DE7 3ET
Tel. 01332-756610

The National Trust   High Peak Estate Office
Edale End, Edale Rd, Hope, via Sheffield S30 2RF
Tel. 01433-70368

British Rail, Hope Valley and Buxton lines
Tel. 0161-234 3157 (Manchester)
Tel. 0114-273 4671/4672 (Sheffield)

OFFERTON MOOR

START *Hathersage*   *Grid ref. SK 231814*

DISTANCE *7½ miles*

ORDNANCE SURVEY MAPS
1:50,000
Landranger 110 - Sheffield & Huddersfield
Landranger 119 - Buxton, Matlock & Dove Dale (just)
1:25,000
Outdoor Leisure 1 - Peak District, Dark Peak
Outdoor Leisure 24 - Peak District, White Peak (just)

ACCESS *Start from the village centre. There is a car park. Served by Sheffield-Castleton buses and a number of less frequent services. Also has its own station on the Hope Valley line (Sheffield-Manchester).*

An airy ramble from the depths of the Derwent Valley to breezy moorland heights, surrounded by a tapestry of outstanding views. For a note on Hathersage please refer to WALK 2.

S Key to this walk is the river Derwent at Leadmill Bridge: while the main road down to the river has a good footway, there is a better alternative. **Leave the junction outside the *George Hotel*, crossing and turning right on Mill Lane alongside the *Little John* pub.** A stream provides company as far as a surviving mill chimney.

The lane passes under the railway viaduct and round to a lodge for Nether Hall. Here take a stile alongside and head down the fieldside on a broad track, keeping straight on down to the corner when the track goes right of barns. The path then runs on through the fields to meet the road at Leadmill Bridge. Looking downstream, the quarried face of Millstone Edge rises boldly up to the left. If desperate, there's a pub just a hundred yards over the bridge!

Cross the bridge and turn upstream. Just past the weir, at an old fence-stile, bear left to find a clear path climbing the steep little wooded bank. Emerging at the top go right on the wallside above the trees, keeping straight on the green way as it rises through the field to the isolated house ahead, there joining a drive. Pause to savour a smashing prospect over the Derwent Valley and above Hathersage to the long skyline of Stanage Edge, and up-dale to Kinder Scout peeking between Lose Hill and Win Hill; Bamford Edge also makes its presence known.

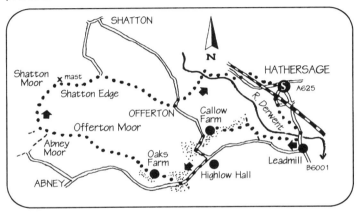

Turn right down the drive towards Broadhay Farm. Over a bridge, turn left through a gate and up to the far end of the 'island' pasture between woods. At the top a stile sees us into the trees and a broad track heads away. At a fork take the path climbing right, to run along the top of the wood. It exits at a small gate in the wall, to climb steeply to emerge onto a drive alongside Callow House. Look back again for those views, with Higger Tor and Millstone Edge also well seen above Hathersage.

Head away up the drive to run on to join a back road. Go left on this traffic-free route through colourful country towards another road. At a bend before the junction a short-cut little rough lane on the right cuts through onto this road, opposite Highlow Hall. This imposing manor house dates from the 16th century, and was once owned by the locally influential Roman Catholic Eyre family. It is said that in the 15th century Robert Eyre built a hall for each of his seven sons, all

13

within a stone's throw at Hazelford, North Lees, Crookhill, Shatton, Moorseats, Nether Shatton, and Offerton. The latter is passed later in this walk. Today Highlow Hall takes in paying guests.

Turn right on the road for another peaceful stroll. Now we have the charms of the deep side valley of Highlow Brook to enjoy, dense bracken flanks rising onto Eyam Moor. Upstream Bretton Clough forges into a wooded defile. **Passing in and out of woods take a stile on the right and head up the pasture on a broad track, with Oaks Farm in view ahead. At a fork take the more inviting lower branch, becoming fainter as it runs on by a wall and up to a corner stile above a wood. Quickly emerging, rise up to meet the farm drive, and go right towards the farm gate.**

Offerton Hall and the Derwent Valley

Don't enter but rise away left on a delectable bracken path. Quickly reaching a crossroads with a broader way, keep straight on up the now thinner path. This slants unerringly across the bracken moor to reach a 'clearing' at a wall corner. On again, a short spell of over exuberant bracken is soon relieved by the increasing presence of heather, and the going constantly eases and improves. Ahead is the sweep of Abney Moor, possibly with gliders high above; note also the parallel lines of the old field walls above Abney Grange.

Keep straight on over a path crossroads, and our way is soon joined by a wall and runs gloriously on this heather covered moor. At the end a fence guides us on to join a broad track. Go right, swinging quickly round to the head of Shatton Lane. Several tracks merge here, together descending the firm surface of this grand old lane. The views are quite stunning in their extent, looking over the Hope Valley to the Mam Tor ridge backed by Kinder Scout, then Win Hill with the Ladybower dam and Bamford Edge rolling into place. Down to our left is the colourful clough of Over Dale. The lane levels out to run on past the BBC mast beneath Shatton Edge, then drops steeply and more roughly again.

A sweeping panorama stretching from Millstone Edge to Mam Tor must rank as one of the Peak's finest! Through a gate on a bend the lane becomes surfaced. Take the ladder-stile in front and head away on a green path across the bottom of Offerton Moor. This runs on to a wall corner. Ignore a branch climbing right and use the wallside path. This combination leads faithfully all the way down the moor, a super path in surroundings to match. At the end it runs on to join the back road (used earlier) above Offerton. Offerton Hall is a splendid old house in a setting to match. Again, once owned by the Eyres, it dates from the mid-16th century with additions a century later. It also supports a fine range of outbuildings. For a fine view of the old house go up the road for a minute or so. Our route turns down, winding between Offerton Hall and Offerton House.

Below the buildings take a gate on the right and a faint grassy way curves down to a stile/gate. This same path runs down the fields to gain the riverbank at a set of stepping stones. The splendid old path was built to link the hall with Hathersage via the stepping stones. Almost three dozen reliable stones convey us across to the opposite bank. If the river is in spate and repels attempts at crossing, then simply turn downstream to trace the river back to Leadmill Bridge.

Having crossed, turn downstream for a pleasant riverbank amble. All too soon a guidepost sends us sharply up a fence side to join the A625. Cross to a stile and slant up to cross the railway line with caution. Slant up a couple more small enclosures to join a back road on the edge of the village, and go right. This road is Jaggers Lane, which with Cogger Lane branching off it recalls the historic importance of these ways, both references to the men who led pack-ponies across the hills. Stay on the road to descend back into the village.

2

EYAM MOOR

START *Hathersage*   *Grid ref. SK 231814*

DISTANCE *7 miles*

ORDNANCE SURVEY MAPS
1:50,000
Landranger 110 - Sheffield & Huddersfield
Landranger 119 - Buxton, Matlock & Dove Dale
1:25,000
Outdoor Leisure 1 - Peak District, Dark Peak
Outdoor Leisure 24 - Peak District, White Peak

ACCESS *Start from the village centre. There is a car park. Served by Sheffield-Castleton buses and a number of less frequent services. Also has its own station on the Hope Valley line (Sheffield-Manchester).*

The deep valley of Highlow Brook and the heather heights of Eyam Moor create a fine combination of scenery both near and far.

S Hathersage is a popular village, more for its surroundings than its own inherent appeal: it is certainly not a 'tourist' village in the style of Castleton. Hathersage is perhaps best known as the former home of Little John, and a gravestone in the churchyard is said to mark the last resting place of Robin Hood's lieutenant. Set back from the main street is the neat St. Michael's Catholic church of 1806, which replaced a 1692 chapel destroyed by local mobs.

Most attractive architecturally of several pubs is the *George Hotel*. Alongside is a rare preserved cheese press, while the junction outside boasts a fine old roadsign-cum-lamp standard. The church of St. Michael & All Angels occupies a lofty eminence above the village. The 14th century tower survived mid-19th century restoration, while inside are some outstanding brasses of the once influential Eyre family.

Key to this walk is the river Derwent at Leadmill Bridge: while the main road down to the river has a good footway, a better alternative is described at the identical start to WALK 1. Cross the Derwent and go just as far as the hamlet and *Plough Inn* at Leadmill, then turn up the Abney road on the right. The old sign and water trough are followed almost at once by an old well on the left. **The road climbs steeply away and at the first chance, at a bend, take a level farm drive off to the left. This runs into trees and emerges into a mixed pasture at a cattle-grid. Drop left on a path into the trees, emerging to run along to a stone arched bridge on Highlow Brook.**

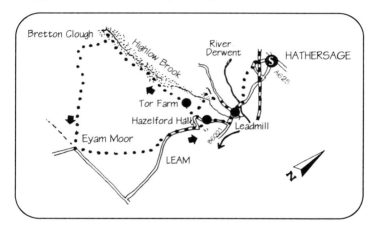

Cross the bridge and climb the wall-side behind, at the top corner joining Hoghall's drive. Continue up to a junction at Leam Lane. Pause to look back over Hathersage and the moors above, with Stanage Edge above Bamford Edge, and Win Hill to their left. **Without joining the road go right on another farm drive. As it drops down to Tor Farm keep straight on through gates in front, and a fine green track runs along the base of a bracken bank. Remain on this same track as it runs on through a couple of fields, just above Highlow Wood to enter a young plantation at a stile at the end.**

A path runs on above the brook to emerge in similar fashion at a ford, path junction and guidepost. Take the unsightly bulldozed track left, leaving the trees behind to rise through bracken. Easing out, the track resumes climbing as our more inviting path branches off right.

17

This is the summit of the path, and free of that track this is a fine place to pause for a while. Frustratingly, initially, the path now proceeds to slant back down, but in lovely surrounds. It passes through forlorn gateposts, into a tiny clough then into trees again to return to the brook at Stoke Ford. This is marked by an incongruous modern footbridge and an historic guidepost. No less than five paths meet at this once important ford, which survives despite the footbridge. This peaceful setting at the confluence of the Bretton and Abney brooks is a hugely colourful scene and, again, a place to linger.

Old guidepost, Stoke Ford

PEAK DISTRICT & NORTHERN COUNTIES FOOTPATHS PRESERVATION SOCIETY 1939

NO. 99 PUBLIC ⇒

FOOTPATH

BY GOTHERAGE BARN TO GRINDLEFORD AND TO EYAM.

LEAVE NO LITTER

Don't cross the brook but bear left back up the slope. Within a minute leave the upstream path and fork left up a steeper, thinner one, which quickly doubles back out of the trees. At the top of the bank the improved path climbs through bracken to the wall above. Going right with it the gradient eases, and the super prospect ahead is further improved just beyond an intervening wall/stile. At a corner we are suddenly placed atop a modest gritstone outcrop on a sharp bend overlooking a glorious prospect of Bretton Clough (illustrated on page 77).

Resuming, the next fine prospect is already upon us, in the form of the rich heather carpet of Eyam Moor in front. Within a minute our broad path puts us onto the bottom corner of the moor. Climbing away, the path at once splits into three. Take the left branch, rising above a wall and quickly joining it to climb up the moor. The heather

moor extends on both sides of the wall, and our return route is somewhere over there. As the gradient eases the path enjoys a fine march to join a road at a 1933 guidepost. Across the Derwent Valley, Froggatt and Curbar edges form a long skyline, while just over to our right is the chimney of the old Ladywash mine.

Eyam is ahead on the road, but we simply go left a few yards to another stile back onto the moor. A path heads away with a fence until the fields draw the fence away and we march on through the heart of the moor. This is a grand stride, gradually working downhill and enjoying increasing views. Hathersage Moor features strongly with Higger Tor, Carl Wark and Burbage Rocks behind; the high moorland of White Edge rises behind Froggatt Edge; while the Derwent Valley below is resplendent in its wooded cloak. Scattered around the moor are dozens of small-scale Bronze Age burial cairns, mostly indistinguishable in the heather. **Towards the end the path drops more steeply to run on to a stile off the moor onto Leam Lane.**

Go left for a few minutes to a sharp bend, and take a stile in the low wall in front. A super view awaits, with Hazelford Hall as a fine foreground. **A faint, initially sunken way descends the pasture to short-cut the road, regaining it alongside Hazelford Hall.** This is a grand 17th century house with mullioned windows in its gable, and was one of many in the Hathersage area owned by the influential Eyre family. **Continue down the narrow lane to quickly join the B6001. Leadmill is just a minute to the left along the good footway, where the floral and more importantly thirst-quenching delights of the** *Plough Inn* **await. Return to Hathersage over the bridge.**

Across the Derwent Valley from Eyam Moor,
looking to Stanage Edge, Higger Tor and Hathersage Moor

19

3

WIN HILL

START Hope   Grid ref. SK 171834

DISTANCE 5 miles

ORDNANCE SURVEY MAPS
1:50,000
Landranger 110 - Sheffield & Huddersfield
1:25,000
Outdoor Leisure 1 - Peak District, Dark Peak

ACCESS Start from the village centre. There is a car park on the main street. Served by Castleton buses from almost anywhere within reason, with regular services from Sheffield, Chesterfield and Bakewell. It also has its own station on the Sheffield-Manchester railway line.

An uncomplicated ascent of a popular landmark, with outstanding views of high moors, gritstone edges and lush valleys. From the very car park the boss of rock crowning our objective beckons alluringly above its lower slopes.

S Hope is a busy village set where its own valley merges with the Vale of Edale. Several pubs and cafes offer refreshment and attempt to waylay those bound for the more regular haunts of nearby Castleton and Edale. Entirely dominant is St. Peter's church, which dates back, in parts, to the 12th century and sends a solid spire towering into the skies. Just outside the church door is an intricately carved 11th century Saxon cross shaft. The 18th century Old Hall is now an inn of that name.

Leave the village centre by the main road (Station Road) east. On the edge of the village we pass an old milestone, advising distances to Castleton, Chapel, Sheffield and Hathersage. **Crossing the bridge**

over the Noe after the last houses, turn left up traffic-free Aston Lane. Immediately under the railway bridge take a stile set back on the right and head across the field. From the top corner continue past a 'baker's dozen' stand of trees to the next stile, then straight across again to reach a path crossroads in front of a tiny footbridge. Here turn left, bound for Win Hill. Appropriately enough, Win Hill's knobbly crest beckons, high on the skyline above.

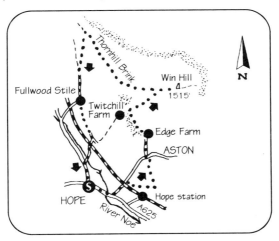

A good path climbs the fieldsides, encountering numerous stiles before emerging onto a rough back road on the edge of Aston. Along to the right is Aston Hall, dated 1578. Go left a few yards then turn right to commence a steep climb up an access road. Rising past King's Haigh it arrives beneath Edge Farm. Straight in front is an old well. Here go left up an enclosed way rising between woodland and old walls. This fine path slants up past a barn to arrive at another path crossroads above Twitchill Farm. Here the direct path from Hope intersects our bridleway.

This is a grand place to break the climb to savour an outstanding view. Looking over Hope and its valley to the Mam Tor-Lose Hill ridge, the latter peak makes a proud sentinel overlooking the meeting of Edale and Hope vales. To its north, the broad shoulders of Kinder Scout form a more sombre but equally impressive picture. Without advancing further, turn sharply right to climb the pasture to a stile onto the open country of **Win Hill. A well worn path slants right through heather and gorse, rising past a cairn by an old wall with the knobbly summit now in view. The going eases on what is by now a complete heather carpet, and the path runs on to meet the permissive ridgetop path. Two minutes to the right, and the summit at 1515ft/462m is underfoot.** A direct branch breaks off to offer a simple scramble to a suitable conclusion.

The top - Win Hill Pike - is marked by an Ordnance Survey column (S4228) and is a hugely popular place. Not surprisingly, there are truly outstanding views over much of the Peak from these idyllic outcrops amongst the heather. Derwent Edge impresses high above the tentacle arms of Ladybower Reservoir (with both viaducts in view); Woodlands Valley leads the eye up to the brooding mass of Bleaklow; Stanage and the eastern edges recede beyond the Derwent Valley; while Offerton and neighbouring moors rise across the nearer Hope Valley.

On the summit of Win Hill, looking to Mam Tor and Rushup Edge

Resume by retracing the ridgetop path, now remaining on it past our entry point for a superb long mile's amble along Thornhill Brink. Easy walking through the heathery expanse leaves ample time to savour the broad views, particularly to Kinder now dominant directly ahead. **A wall comes in for company then disappears again.** Just beyond here is a popular take-off point for paragliders, and their antics in attempting to deal with the thermals might occupy you for some time.

On again, the path descends steadily, ignoring a branch doubling back left at a cairn. We leave the heather behind to pass through an old wall, now with the plantations very close to the right. Just through it is a crossroads of paths. Take that quitting the ridge by doubling sharply back to the left. This slants down beneath the ridge we have traversed, a well made descent on an old sunken way through bracken.

As we lose height, Lose Hill gains in stature across the narrow valley. **At the bottom we meet a broad track.** This bridleway has come over from the Woodlands Valley, having crossed the ridge past Hope Cross (see the companion volume *Northern Peak*). It is the line of the Roman road from MELANDRA (Glossop) to the fort at NAVIO (Brough) near Hope.

At once the track becomes enclosed, upgrading to a rough road as it runs a leafy passage down to a sharp bend in front of Fullwood Stile Farm. Go straight ahead, right of the main buildings and alongside them to a stile on the right. The path then crosses a couple of fieldtops to reach a lone house. Continue along its drive, emerging into a lane which descends beneath the railway. Here at Earle Sidings the short branch to the Hope Valley cement works departs.

The lane runs out to a very attractive corner at Killhill Bridge. Cross the Noe and up onto the Edale road. Go left, with adjacent footway, for the few minutes back into the village centre.

*Saxon cross shaft,
Hope churchyard*

23

VALE OF EDALE

START *Hope* *Grid ref. SK 171834*

FINISH *Edale*

DISTANCE *5½ miles*

ORDNANCE SURVEY MAPS
1:50,000
Landranger 110 - Sheffield & Huddersfield
1:25,000
Outdoor Leisure 1 - Peak District, Dark Peak

ACCESS *Start from Hope, finish at Edale railway station, both on the Sheffield-Manchester line. If coming by car, it is easier to park in Hope village car park and return from Edale by train. Add an extra half-mile for the walk back into Hope from the station.*

An easy, low level linear walk tracing the river Noe through the portals of Win and Lose Hills into the fair Vale of Edale.

The Hope Valley line was completed in 1894 by the Midland Railway, another Sheffield-Manchester link joining its far older trans-Pennine cousin, the Woodhead line through Longdendale. Though that line was discarded, this happily survives to serve some of the best walking country in the Peak. For a note on Hope please refer to WALK 3.

S **Leave the village by the main road (Station Road) east.** On the edge of the village an old milestone advises distances to Castleton, Chapel, Sheffield and Hathersage. **Across the bridge on the river Noe take a stile on the left and head upstream through the fields.** Win Hill's steep slopes dominate to the right. **On reaching a former mill the path drops down into its yard.** Note the iron waterwheel on the left. **Follow the drive out to the road at Killhill Bridge.**

Across the bridge a tiny short-cut path leads up onto the Edale road. Turn right for a short half-mile, a footway materialises to ease progress. En route we pass the *Cheshire Cheese,* an attractive 16th century pub, and under a viaduct carrying a short branch from the Hope Valley cement works: its lack of character is in keeping with its purpose. On a happier note the cone of Lose Hill is directly ahead.

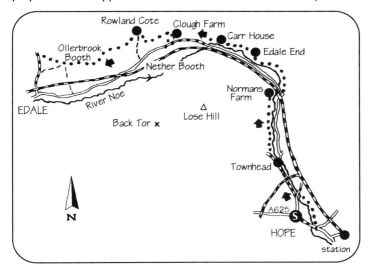

At Townhead bear left on a 'no through road' before the main road drops to cross the river. At the first chance (starting to climb) take a stile on the right and head off along the field. This runs on close to the river, tending to keep a more direct line slightly above the bank of the winding river. At various places Lose Hill makes a fine peak immediately above us. **The way runs on to curve around to Normans Farm. Keep right of the buildings and double back out on the drive. This crosses the river as it emerges from beneath the rail line, and we rejoin the Edale road again.**

Pass under the rail bridge and briefly along the road before a stile and gate on the right send us off. The path emerges into a field, and at the far end enters woodland. This is the finest section as a super path (a short section of which is permissive) runs on through lovely beechwood on the riverbank, with the modest stream enjoying a mini-gorge for a spell. **At the other end we emerge to enter the Vale of Edale proper.** This second half of the walk ushers us into the 'promised land', with the bulky shoulders of Kinder Scout arrayed across the dale. **Follow the riverbank to reach Bagshaw Bridge and turn right up the drive to Edale End.** Here the National Trust has its High Peak estate office and wardens' workshop. There is also an information shelter.

At the farm bridge go left towards the Upper Fulwood farmyard, but look out for a stile on the left which is the first of several sending us round the outside of the buildings. At the far end advance to the winding river and on to a stile. Joining a broad track follow this on through the field centre to the houses at Carr House ahead. Go right of the first house to follow the track on to the second, here joining its drive out onto the road. Lose Hill now shows its shadowy northern face, joined by the hugely impressive Back Tor and the Great Ridge along to Mam Tor.

Turn right on the road for half a mile. Make the most of this by enjoying the view across to the afore-mentioned Great Ridge. **Beyond the drive to Clough Farm, on a bend, advance a little further to find a 1905 guidepost sending a bridleway back up to the right. This enclosed leafy way (an historic packhorse route) runs on above Clough Farm.** A more direct but inferior option continues on the road to Nether Booth, just ahead, where a fieldpath heads off for Edale.

Over the stream and gate behind the farm, leave the bridleway and turn up the wallside to an old gate. Rise a little further through bracken to join a broad path. Go left over the stile and follow this wallside path on beneath a bracken pasture. Ahead now is a fine spread of the Vale of Edale, and rounding a corner the scene reaches a crescendo when faced with the colourful prospect of Lady Brook Booth climbing to the Kinder skyline. **The path curves in towards the clough, crossing the stream to arrive at the youth hostel at Rowland Cote.**

Pass along the front of the house and on past the last buildings. At the end of the car park a kissing-gate sends a splendid green path heading away through the fields. A row of hawthorns lead us on to a gorse bank, then the path drops down behind a house. Ahead, the last lap awaits as Edale's church spire protrudes from the trees, while Grindslow Knoll juts into the sky from the face of Kinder Scout. **The fainter path runs on to the fence opposite, then down its near side**

to meet a firm path running through the fields. Go over the stile and follow this right, running on into a drive to enter the characterful hamlet of Ollerbrook Booth.

Keep straight on the rough road between the various buildings, to be faced with a fork in front of the final barn. The left branch is the quickest, obvious route to the station. **For the village centre, the right branch runs on as a firm, broad path to reach Grinds Brook, en route enjoying views up into Grindsbrook Clough. At the stream leave the track and drop down a path into the trees to find a packhorse bridge spanning the brook.** This old bridge served the packhorse route from Edale via Ollerbrook and Nether Booths, up past Clough House to the Jaggers Clough route. **It also rather conveniently leads us to the *Old Nags Head* and the village street. To finish go left down the road to find the railway station.**

Winter in the Vale of Edale: Lose Hill and Back Tor

Edale is a near legendary place, known only to local ramblers until the Pennine Way was deemed to begin its lumbering journey to the Scottish border from here. Despite this fame, one could be forgiven for thinking it has had no effect on the place: stand in the centre and there are the *Old Nag's Head*, school, Post office/shop and some attractive cottages. In truth, not much *has* changed, and tourists can do little more than gawp for five minutes then get on their way.

For walkers however, Edale will always be the major jumping off point for untold excursions onto Kinder Scout: the affinity between the two is in the Matterhorn/Zermatt mould. Quite naturally, therefore, both Edale and Kinder features strongly in the companion book *Northern Peak*. The tall spired church of the Holy and Undivided Trinity looks down upon this fair scene, which working towards the station also features a National Park Visitor Centre/Mountain Rescue Post, the *Rambler Inn*, (formerly the *Church Inn*) and a tiny cafe.

5

CAVE DALE
& MAM TOR

START *Castleton*   *Grid ref. SK 149829*

DISTANCE *6½ miles*

ORDNANCE SURVEY MAPS
1:50,000
Landranger 110 - Sheffield & Huddersfield
1:25,000
Outdoor Leisure 1 - Peak District, Dark Peak

ACCESS *Start from the village centre. There is a large car park. Served by bus from almost anywhere within reason, with regular services from Sheffield, Chesterfield and Bakewell. In addition, Hope station is two miles distant on the Sheffield-Manchester railway line.*

An absorbing approach to one of the Peak's major landmarks.

⑤ For a note on Castleton please refer to WALK 6. **Leave the main street by Castle Street, rising past a couple of pubs and the church to the Market Place.** Historic Castleton Hall, a youth hostel, stands back on the right. **Bear left on Pindale Road rising above the green, and a little higher, look for a path up to the right between houses. At once it enters the dark walls guarding the entrance to Cave Dale.**

A broad path rises into this deep amphitheatre, a green bowl overlooked by limestone tors. The stony path runs up the floor of the dry valley to rise out of the head. Look back to appraise a spectacular scene as the keep of Peveril Castle rises majestically above a limestone cliff, itself overtopped by Lose Hill across the valley. Peveril Castle is said to have been built by William Peveril, illegitimate son of William the Conqueror: principal feature is the ruinous keep, added in 1176.

In gentler surrounds the path rises further, as a green carpet along the floor of the upper reach of the valley. Reaching an old iron gate, pass through this and the next one. Beyond here, the bridlepath slants left up the gentle brow, over to the far corner. A tiny enclosed way leads onto a rough road. Turn right along this, and at the first bend go straight ahead on the pleasanter wall-side track up the rough pasture. Over to the right rises Mam Tor, not appearing much higher than our already elevated position.

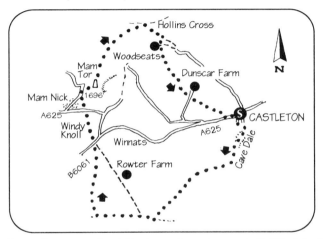

At the wall crossroads at the top a branch goes left. We take the pathless branch right, rising with the wall above old mine workings on this rough pasture. Views south-west lead towards Buxton and its bowl of moors. A thin path forms and shadows the wall over the brow. Ahead, Mam Tor lines up with Rushup Edge, backed by Kinder Scout's southern skyline; to the right is a long skyline of Derwent Edge beyond Back Tor, Lose Hill and Win Hill. Dropping gently down, a large pasture is entered. Part way down, the delectable green path leaves the wall to cross to the far corner, clearly bound for Mam Tor. Here it meets the Rowter farm drive as it joins the B6061.

Go right a few yards and take a gate/stile opposite. A track traces the wallside and continues on through the pasture of Windy Knoll to a stile onto the A625. Excavations at Windy Knoll Cave have yielded remains of Iron Age mammals. The busy car park to the left usually boasts a snack bar. Cross straight over and up the slope to meet the

road on the crest of Mam Nick. By now the Hope Valley is outspread as on a map, but as we start to climb, it is the northerly prospect that grabs attention. Here Kinder Scout spreads its all embracing shoulders around the Vale of Edale, with Edale village nestling in the folds of Grinds Brook.

Without setting foot on the road a made path rises parallel with it, quickly turning right to breast the slopes of Mam Tor. The way (steps then flags) leads unerringly and quickly to the stone built Ordnance Survey column (S4230) at 1696ft/517m. Mam Tor is commonly known as the 'Shivering Mountain', a reference to the alarmingly unstable face it presents to the Hope Valley. The shaley slopes (sandstone alternating with layers of 'mudstone') have seen numerous landslips at times of severe weather. The last one was the final straw for the A623 along its flank: the road was destroyed and left to the elements. That gap on the map is just what it looks like, though light traffic still has the use of the Winnats Pass to link the Hope Valley with Chapel-en-le-Frith and points west.

This is unquestionably a classic Peakland viewpoint, but one must nevertheless move a few yards to bring in more intimate valley views to join the likes of Kinder, the ridge to Lose Hill, and the Derwent edges. Visitors stood on its broad summit would do well to remember the lethal drop awaiting from the hill's east face, particularly the tourist wandering casually up from Mam Nick car park: beware strong winds! By veering a little to the north we can look down on the very well defined ramparts that once helped defend a possibly 3000 year old, 16 acre Iron Age hillfort on the summit.

The flagged path continues down the other side, returning to the eroded path as it runs along the ridge to Hollins Cross. A memorial cairn marks this junction of modern ways overlaying old packhorse routes. Ahead, Back Tor and Lose Hill invite a longer traverse, and there is little to deter such a route change: simply turn to WALK 6 at Hollins Cross and read on from there.

Our less ambitious way quits the ridge at this point, turning down the worn slanting path to the right. This descends roughly to a stile, and then down further colourful terrain. If followed to the bottom it leads to a lanehead, joining a farm road becoming surfaced to lead all the way back to the village as Hollowford Road. This is the way most folk seem to go, but a far nicer route awaits.

Before the bottom of the rough path, take a more inviting one slanting more gently down to the right, and in the corner it meets the drive just short of Woodseats Farm. Cross straight over to another stile and down the fieldside, with a line of occasional trees in the next field leading to another fieldside. Ahead is the dark hole of Peak Cavern on the edge of Castleton. **Reaching a small wood, turn right down to a couple of stiles in front and resume with the trees on the left. From a stile at the end cross to a stile onto a narrow farm road.**

Cross over by the cattle-grid and resume down the fieldside with a tiny stream, Odin Sitch. Ahead is the castle keep, while around to the right the limestone tors of the Winnats lead the eye back up to our ridge. **This pleasant finish passes through stiles and concludes by crossing to the end of a tapering field, where a short snicket leads out between houses onto the village street.**

*Peveril Castle
and Mam Tor*

6

LOSE HILL

START *Castleton*   *Grid ref. SK 149829*

DISTANCE *6½ miles*

ORDNANCE SURVEY MAPS
1:50,000
Landranger 110 - Sheffield & Huddersfield
1:25,000
Outdoor Leisure 1 - Peak District, Dark Peak

ACCESS *Start from the village centre, there is a good sized car park. Served by bus from almost anywhere within reason, with regular services from Sheffield, Chesterfield and Bakewell. In addition, Hope station is 2 miles distant on the Sheffield-Manchester railway line.*

A classic walk in the Hope Valley, accessing the Great Ridge by way of some lesser used paths in amongst the more obvious ridgepaths.

S Castleton is a hugely popular village, a major tourist draw thanks to its beautiful location, attractive centre and numerous surrounding features. Of these the showcaves are pre-eminent, and with no less than four to choose from, few visitors go home without sampling one. Treak Cliff, Blue John, Peak and Speedwell Caverns all offer much to see of the great underworld: the latter is a former lead mine and claims the novelty of taking you deep underground by boat.

All the caves have impressive stalactite and stalagmite formations, with Treak Cliff and Blue John renowned for their Blue John veins. Nearest to the village - virtually in it - is Peak Cavern, which boasts an immense entrance hole. This mineral is said to be unique to the area, and the village gift shops will try to ensure you take a fashioned piece of the stone home with you. It is claimed to have been mined by the Romans as a diversion from lead mining, though evidence is lacking.

No-one can fail to be impressed by the setting of Peveril Castle overlooking the village from a near vertical, easily defended knoll. It is in the care of English Heritage and the steep climb is worth the effort. It is said to have been built by William Peveril, illegitimate son of William the Conqueror, and the principal feature is the ruinous keep which was added in 1176.

St. Edmund's church is centrally placed by the Market Place, and though restored in the 19th century it boasts a Norman arch and some superb 17th century dated box pews. Across the square is Castleton Hall, dating in part from the 17th century and now serving as a youth hostel. A museum dedicated to local life and tradition is located in the old Methodist church school. Pubs and cafes offer refreshments galore, and there is an information centre in Castle Street.

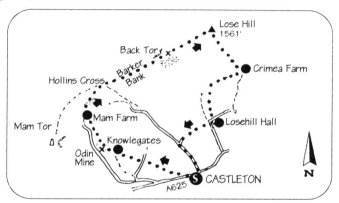

Head west along the street as far as the entrance to Peak Cavern at the edge of the village. Just beyond it, locate a narrow snicket on the right between houses, emerging into a field. Bear left with the wall to the end, then trace the trickle of Odin Sitch upstream through the fields to join a farm road by a cattle-grid. Directly above us, Mam Tor impresses greatly, with the Winnats to its left and the ridge continuing east to our objectives, Back Tor and Lose Hill.

Cross the road and up the fieldside, veering left with the sike. Cross it towards the end to a stile in the wall ahead, and head up the field to a stile in front of farm buildings. An enclosed path runs on to emerge onto the drive in front of the house at Knowlegates Farm.

Go straight across and up round the back of a barn, scaling a bank to a stile into dense bracken. A good grass path rises away through dense, tall bracken (scene of woodland regeneration efforts by the National Trust) to the start of a firm path at some recolonised spoil heaps in the vicinity of the Odin Mine.

Following the main path left into the trees reveals more of this former lead mine. Principal feature is an iron ring 5 yards in diameter, with a smaller one rimming a typical gritstone 'milling' stone still in place on top. It dates from the early 19th century, when a horse would haul the millstone around the great iron ring to crush lead ore. Iron rich water also emerges from a nearby spring. A path then rises to the abandoned Mam Tor road, from where successive right turns lead back onto our main route at Mam Farm.

The Odin Mine, looking to Mam Tor

Our chosen way forks right at the spoil heaps, eschewing the good path and bending round the back of the spoil to a pair of step-stiles in fences. Amidst more dense bracken an improving path heads away, bound for Mam Farm ahead. As the bracken falls away the path curves round to the farm. A stile up to the left admits onto the drive. Don't go into the yard but take the drive behind the buildings.

As the drive winds round with another house up ahead, take a stile on the left from where a path climbs steeply away. Walkers often appear as silhouettes on the ridge high above. The path passes

34

through youthful mixed woodland above the house then slants up a couple of colourful open pastures to gain the ridge at Hollins Cross. A memorial cairn marks this junction of modern ways overlaying old packhorse routes. This is a supreme moment as Kinder Scout and the Vale of Edale appear dramatically in front: a classic scene!

Turn right along the busy path on the crest of Barker Bank. Note that the public path actually contours along the slope to the right, beneath us, and offers a splendid crowd-free alternative along to the next saddle, losing little in views as the ridge wall in any case interrupts the Kinder scene. Looking back, it is easy to appraise the contouring defensive wall of Mam Tor's Iron Age hillfort, a site which covered 16 acres.

At the next dip the path runs on to beneath the awesome Back Tor, and a couple of paths merge from the right. Cross a stile and climb the roughly eroded path onto the crest of the rocks. This lofty eminence is a famous landmark and a grand place to be, offering another magic moment from its rocky platform (take care with young 'uns on the edge). The view back along to Mam Tor and Rushup Edge is a superb addition to the further improved Kinder prospect. Directly opposite is the farming hamlet of Nether Booth, with the red roof of Rowland Cote youth hostel up the clough behind: various other cloughs and knolls abound.

From Back Tor it is but a few minutes further to a short climb onto Lose Hill, entering National Trust land at a stile from where a flagged path leads to the summit. The top of Lose Hill is crowned by a splendid topograph identifying many features of interest in the wonderful view. The ground falls away quite steeply to north and east, affording a good prospect of the curving course of the river Noe and attendant railway as it wriggles out from the Vale of Edale and beneath the slopes of Win Hill. Lose Hill's upper reaches are also known as Ward's Piece, in memory of stalwart veteran access campaigner G.H.B. Ward.

Leave by the other built path heading south, dropping steeply to a stile out of National Trust land. Bear right to a stile in the fence just below, then turn downhill with the fence. Very quickly a well-worn path forms, and drops pleasantly down towards Crimea Farm (Losehill Farm on maps). Just above it, a permissive path is signed off the path, down to a ladder-stile in the corner. If seeking refreshment, however, continue down to the farm where you will find Losehill Larder purveying refreshments. Additionally, it features hand crafted gifts, spinning demonstrations and a family farm trail.

From the stile drop down the fieldside to a pair of stiles where the farm detour comes in. Go right across the field centre, a track forming to become enclosed at the end. When it turns down to Spring House Farm, take the stile in front and resume along the field top. At the end another track is joined and followed down towards Riding House Farm. At a kink just before it, take a stile in front and go down the fieldside with a tree lined stream. At the bottom corner a shady dell is entered and the stream crossed. Climb to a stile and then down a couple of fieldsides to join a back lane.

Go right on here, along the rear of Losehill Hall. Built in 1882 by a local lead mining magnate, it has for many years operated as the Peak National Park Study Centre. On offer is an extensive programme of outdoor oriented, environmentally aware courses, either week-long or weekends, and also holidays. **At the bend, the drive goes left and out onto the road at the edge of the village. An alternative takes the stile straight ahead, and along a fieldside to a stile and trickle stream. Cross to a stile in a corner opposite to join a drive. Go ahead on this to meet Hollowford Lane alongside Hollowford training centre. Turn left along here to return to the village centre.** En route, a curious circle of five stones stand in an enclosure on the right.

Back Tor

36

7

HAY DALE
& DAM DALE

START *Peak Forest*   *Grid ref. SK 113792*

DISTANCE *6½ miles*

ORDNANCE SURVEY MAPS
1:50,000
Landranger 119 - Buxton, Matlock & Dove Dale
1:25,000
Outdoor Leisure 24 - Peak District, White Peak

ACCESS *Start from the pub in the village centre. There is parking on Church Lane just off the A623, opposite the church. Served by Tideswell to Chapel-en-le-Frith buses usually operating from more distant Chesterfield and Stockport.*

Old lead mining pastures on the way out, unassuming dry limestone dales on the return; Wheston and its historic cross midway.

S Astride a busy highway, Peak Forest's name recalls the medieval Royal Forest of the Peak that spread over much of north-western Peakland. Centrepiece is the church, the unusually dedicated King Charles the Martyr, rebuilt around 1880. The village pub is the *Devonshire Arms,* and there is a Post office/shop on Church Lane.

Head east on the main road, grateful for the footway until its abrupt premature end. Immediately after the last building on the left, step over the low wall and head across the hollowed field centre. From the corner stile go left with the wall, the nick in the skyline ahead being our objective. Crossing a couple more stiles rise up past a path crossroads to beneath a lone house, where a stile crosses the wall and just further up another stile empties onto a back road.

Go right as far as a bend. Just before this is Brecktor Farm, where liquid refreshment may be on offer. **At the bend go straight ahead over a couple of stiles and a green way heads off. This is a former miners' track serving the distinctly mining environs of this pasture.** Strictly the path crosses to a stile on the left, up to a gateway and then back down to recross the wall by a ladder-stile alongside a reedy pond. **In practise it is easier to keep straight on the green track below an upright millstone to a gateway by which time the right of way has returned. Don't advance on to Wheston House Farm ahead, but bear right to locate a midway stile onto a road.**

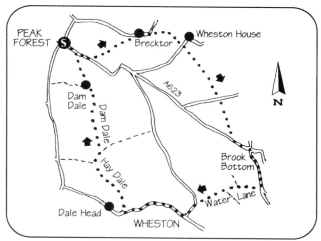

Crossing straight over to another stile, bear left down the field. Here we cross the assumed line of Batham Gate Roman road linking Buxton and Brough. **Pass a dewpond to a stile midway down. Cross two fields diagonally to corner stiles, then down the wall-side to the next corner.** All this was once Tideswell Moor. **Now bear gently left to a facing stile onto another back road, Pittlesmere Lane. Again go straight over, down to the far end, through the old wall then left to a stile midway down. One final diagonal leads out onto the A623.**

Go nervously left, grateful for the verge, and escape right at a crossroads, down the road into Brook Bottom. On the right is a lead polluted stream, and a warning advises not to pick the watercress. **At the first chance, as trees are met, turn up the unsurfaced Water Lane**

on the right. **This engages a short pull twixt walls then runs broadly on, ignoring two branches and descending Roman-like onto a road. Keep left to descend to the T-junction at Wheston, and directly in front is the Georgian hall. Turn right, and after the first farm building Wheston Cross is to be found on the left.** It stands forlorn in a little enclosure on a two tiered base. The cross itself is thought to date from the 15th century, probably a boundary cross of the deer forest. One side features a crucifixion scene, another the Madonna & Child. **Resume along the road, down into the attractive valley floor at Dale Head. Here Peter Dale runs in from the left to transform into Hay Dale.**

Take the stile on the right into the green floor of Hay Dale. This dry valley is an unassuming gem, not dramatic but nevertheless lovely as we stroll on past old mine workings and beneath a canopy of trees. **At the end turn right on a rough lane, leaving at the first chance by a stile sending us on into Dam Dale. Even gentler than Hay Dale, the way remains clear as we run along the base of the slope on the right. When Dam Dale Farm appears ahead keep faith with the wall (not as per map), curving round along the well defined base of the slope to arrive level with the farm. Pass through the bridle-gate and on to a corner stile, thus having completely avoided the farm environs.**

Cross straight over the low brow to the next stile. Immediately above a lone house down to the left is the grassy embankment of an old dam. **With Peak Forest appearing just ahead, keep straight on to another stile and guidepost at a crossroads of paths. Go over the stile and slant gently left down through further stiles to join the left-hand wall below, continuing on to emerge back onto the main road alongside the old village pump. Go left to finish.**

Wheston Cross

39

8

ABNEY MOOR

START *Bradwell*   *Grid ref. SK 174810*

DISTANCE *6¾ miles*

ORDNANCE SURVEY MAPS
1:50,000
Landranger 110 - Sheffield & Huddersfield
Landranger 119 - Buxton, Matlock & Dove Dale
1:25,000
Outdoor Leisure 1 - Peak District, Dark Peak
Outdoor Leisure 24 - Peak District, White Peak

ACCESS *Start from the village centre. Various minor parking places, best being along Brookside just off the main road by the public toilets. Served by Sheffield-Castleton and Tideswell-Castleton buses, and other less frequent services.*

❾ The busy former lead mining community of Bradwell is not a tourist village, but has several claims to fame. Bagshawe Cavern arranges caving adventure trips, while the village's own brand of ice cream is enjoyed throughout the district. A third feature is the cement works, which on the positive side is a useful source of local employment. St. Barnabas' church is 19th century, while there are several pubs and shops.

Leave the main street by Soft Water Lane, which heads east opposite the sign to the toilets on Brookside. After the last houses and a barn, turn through a gap-stile on the right and a path goes off through a small enclosure. Wooded slopes above us lead to Rebellion Knoll high on the skyline. **Continue past a barn group and on through stiles to reach a line of trees. Here the barely discernible path forks. Take the upper one, rising to a kissing-gate then again to a stile in the top corner.**

Just in front of this we pass over the Grey Ditch, an ancient ditch with a high bank: it possibly originated as a defensive line between Britons and Anglian settlers, perhaps 1500 years ago. Ahead, Win Hill is directly in front, with Lose Hill and the Mam Tor ridge further west. **From the stile pass along the base of a gorse bank to join a farm road on a hairpin bend. Go right on this along to Bothams Farm. Without entering take a stile on the right, then along the field bottom to one in the corner. Climb to a stile in front, from where an inviting green path slants up the pasture.** Fine views are now enjoyed over the Hope Valley to Win and Lose Hills, though there's no avoiding the cement works! **Easing out, the path runs on to a gate onto Brough Lane.**

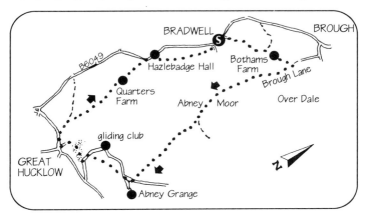

Turn right up this enclosed rough road, which slowly eases out to run an increasingly pleasant course. On the right we pass the upper section of the Grey Ditch in the field, while over to the left Shatton Moor heaves its bulkier frame above the impressive clough of Over Dale. **Derbyshire Wildlife Trust's Over Dale nature reserve is passed on the left to reach a multiple wall junction at a gate. The old road then runs on into the dense bracken of Abney Moor.**

Within a hundred yards branch off it on a well marked path at a stile on the right. This runs on across a modest moorland amphitheatre, a delectable green way through the bracken. Offerton Moor remains to the left with Eyam Moor ahead beyond Bretton Clough. **From the brow at the far end the bracken recedes and our path gently descends to meet a road above Abney Grange.**

41

Turn right just as far as the farm drive and take a stile in front, at the junction. Over to the right the gliding club is evident above the road. **Cross to the far corner of the field and descend with a wall to a tiny stream, heading away again to a ladder-stile at the end.** From its top look back down the upper reaches of Bretton Clough, noting in particular an old landslip on the opposite side. **A faint way curves round the pasture to drop to a waterworks building at the head of the clough, then climb through a couple of fields to rejoin the road we left earlier.**

Go left into the trees, then as it swings away double back on a thin path on the right. This is actually an old byway, and as it forges into the trees it broadens out before descending to a lanehead at a school. Just beneath us the village of Great Hucklow is well camouflaged in greenery, and the lane drops down to enter the village street: turn right. Features of interest all arrayed on the left are the Methodist Chapel of 1806; a fine three storey Georgian house; the Unitarian conference and holiday centre; and the village pub, the *Queen Anne.* The right side boasts a well maintained linear green, complete with seats.

Just past the pub, on the edge of the village, a junction of ways meet at a triangle of rough ground. Take that bearing right, with a pairing of de-restriction and 'unsuitable for motors' signs making unlikely bedfellows. Our rough road drops gently away, crossing over a mine road (serving Milldam Mine fluorspar works) before running more happily away.

A little after this interruption a more inviting track heads away from a gate on the right. Over to the left is the prominent huddle of cottages at Little Hucklow, while up above us is the steep sweep of the edge: here gliders are likely to be seen soaring above on any decent weekend.

The track runs on through a colourful scrub bank. As it turns to swing up to a modern house, keep straight on to a stile by a gate ahead and remain on a good track. A little further this too swings up to the right, bound for the old washing plant it once served. Again go straight on, locating a corner stile then along a rough field top to the far end. Down below is another active mine. **From the corner stile slant down the large field in the company of a fence, bound for Quarters Farm immediately in front.**

Maintain this course to arrive above a little clough with a wall-stile just ahead. Advance to the farm, keeping left of all buildings to a gate onto its drive. Head away on this to emerge onto the B6049, and go right just as far as the farm at Hazlebadge Hall. Hazlebadge Hall once belonged to Haddon Hall, and sports the Vernon coat of arms dated 1549 above the mullioned windows of its prominent western gable.

Gable end, Hazlebadge Hall

Between Hall Farm and Hazlebadge Hall turn up a narrow green way behind a barn. At the top this joins a track above the farm buildings. Don't follow it but bear left over the brow of the domed pasture, on the top passing a mineral vein that is being partly exploited. Pass through an old gateway and down the centre of the pasture towards the houses of Bradwell, reaching a stile in the wall just in front of them. Walk down the street to the Green, then bear left to find a flight of steps by a Victorian postbox, descending onto Church Street and an enclosed village green. Arriving rather neatly opposite the *Valley Lodge*, an award winning pub, go right past the parish church to conclude.

9

TIDESWELL DALE & MILLER'S DALE

START *Tideswell* *Grid ref. SK 153741*

DISTANCE *5 miles*

ORDNANCE SURVEY MAPS
1:50,000
Landranger 119 - Buxton, Matlock & Dove Dale
1:25,000
Outdoor Leisure 24 - Peak District, White Peak

ACCESS *Start from the National Park's Tideswell Dale car park, half a mile south of the village on the B6049. Alternatively start from the village centre. Tideswell is served by bus from numerous places, most notably Sheffield, Chesterfield, Buxton and Bakewell, and many of these also pass through Tideswell Dale and Miller's Dale.*

A limestone gem, with bundles of interest centred on the river Wye and Miller's Dale area.

S **Leave the car park by the footpath past the toilets, descending into Tideswell Dale's limestone recesses.** The dale is owned by the National Park, and the first section offers wheelchair access. All around is delightful greenery with scars and cliffs unfolding. **Cross at a footbridge or wait until the second one.** Up above is Ravenstor youth hostel, while we penetrate an increasingly ravine-like valley.

This charming walk ends at a small parking area on the little road into Litton Mill, with the river Wye in front. Go left for two minutes in the company of the river to enter the hamlet. Litton Mill is also featured on page 80. **Opposite the tearooms turn right on a short path to a footbridge over the river. A path climbs the wooded bank to join the**

Monsal Trail. For more on this trail, see WALK 19. **Go right under the bridge and through a cutting to chug merrily along.** A break in the trees offers a fine chance to look over to the impressive limestone face of Ravens Tor, on the roadside by the river. **At a crossroads with a footpath, an information board on the left gives the option of a modest detour (less than a mile) on a concession path.** A leaflet *Miller's Dale Quarry Nature Reserve* can be obtained at National Park Centres to add to your enjoyment.

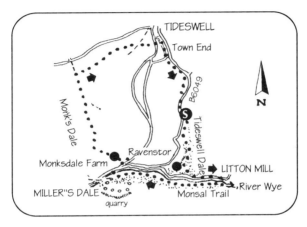

The concession path enjoys a little circuit on the southern flank of the dale, focal point being a vast old quarry. The path climbs to a stile then slants up open pasture to the old quarries. A dangerous crack made the quarry wall unsafe, causing it to be abandoned in 1930. This spot also marks a good viewpoint, looking over the main valley and up Monk's Dale. White topped marker posts send the path along the front through a network of grassed-over spoil heaps, forging on until a footpath junction. The main path doubles back down to the right to rejoin the trail alongside some old limekilns.

Miller's Dale limeworks operated from 1878 to 1930 to provide quicklime for both industry and agriculture, where it helped sweeten acidic land). These massive specimens feature four great arches dwarfed by the whole structure. Charged with crushed limestone and coal, this was burned in the kilns to produce the quicklime which was then taken away by rail. Enforced closure of the quarry above also brought the kilns' operation to a premature end. Miller's Dale Nature Reserve is owned by the National Park and managed by Derbyshire Wildlife Trust. **Next objective is the *Anglers Rest* pub in Miller's Dale, below. Those not undertaking the trail simply descend the path on the right to a footbridge on the Wye. Those ending the trail at the kilns return to the path junction. Either way, descend to the river, its footbridge leading across to the start of the side road into Litton Mill, by the pub.**

The Wye at Litton Mill

Just yards to the left before the junction an iron waterwheel is still in situ. Ahead, St. Anne's church of 1880 slots neatly into the limited space available in this pokey corner. **A flight of steps at the side of the pub lead up to the B6049, and just to the left a narrow back road climbs steeply away. Turn up this, leaving at the first opportunity by a track along to the left. This rises to Monksdale Farm.** The farm stands on the site of a grange of Lenton Abbey, near Nottingham. **Turn up the drive the few yards to the farmhouse, and from a gate behind it a green track rises gently away.** There are grand views over to the left of the viaduct, kilns and old quarry high above.

Remain on this track for a considerable time, bending up to the right and gradually levelling out. Down to the left is Monk's Dale, so tightly enclosed it is not well seen. **At a fork of like tracks keep left, running generally level now and in time approaching a house visible ahead. Before this however a prominent stile and guidepost on the right send a path off for the final leg of the walk.**

46

A thin path heads across the field to a corner stile, then up (passing another dewpond) to a prominent one on the brow. **Crossing the green lane, the path bears left through a close series of gap-stiles before resuming a direct line with the wall. Keep straight on with a wall on the left to meet another green lane, Slancote Lane. Again straight over to a slim squeezer, Tideswell quickly appears ahead. Simply descend the wall-side with little gap-stiles hard by to emerge onto a back road.** We have a grand view over the village to the left in the final stage, with the church tower well seen.

Go right a couple of yards and down Primrose Lane, becoming a footway to join another back road, Gordon Road. The *Horse & Jockey* pub is just yards to the left. Either go left for the village centre, or right to return to the start point. Tideswell itself is described in WALK 10. **The back road leads along to a road at the end of the village.** On the right a pinfold for gathering stray farm animals has been transformed into a small garden.

Cross straight over the road and on an improving green lane. On reaching a gate, slip through a gap on the left for a thinner path to run on through undergrowth. It slants down to join the B6049 at a stile, and on with a footway past the sewage works. At the end a path on the other side breaks off to run beneath a fine line of beeches to lead back into the car park.

Limekilns,
Miller's Dale

10

CRESSBROOK DALE

START *Tideswell*   *Grid ref. SK 151755*

DISTANCE *6 (or 4½) miles*

ORDNANCE SURVEY MAPS
1:50,000
Landranger 119 - Buxton, Matlock & Dove Dale
1:25,000
Outdoor Leisure 24 - Peak District, White Peak

ACCESS *Start from the village centre. There is a small car park opposite the tiny Roman Catholic church down the main street, and various roadside parking. Tideswell is served by bus from numerous places, most notably Sheffield, Chesterfield, Buxton and Bakewell. An alternative start from Litton knocks a good 1½ miles off the walk.*

An easy ramble into the hidden delights of a superb dry valley.

S Tideswell is one of the Peak's favourite villages, a buzzing little place of sombre grey-stone buildings. It is dominated by the church of St. John the Baptist, known as the 'Cathedral of the Peak'. This beautiful building dates largely from the 14th century, and there is so much of interest that a leisurely amble is advisable, armed with a brief guide available within. In contrast, the Roman Catholic church of the Sacred Heart of Mary is a tiny, simple place of worship. Numerous shops (including a chippy) and pubs line the main street in the village centre, with the *George Hotel* (an 18th century coaching inn) occupying prime position alongside the church: a classic arrangement.

Leave the main street opposite the *George*, by a short way between houses that climbs a bank, becoming a snicket to rise onto Church Lane overlooking the village. Head away along this quiet, narrow road to quickly descend into Litton.

Litton is a very attractive village, its houses lining a wide street set back from a spacious green. The main green features the old stocks and ancient tiered cross base, complemented by the pub, the *Red Lion*. Christ Church dates only from 1927, but look for the Clergy House of 1723. There is also a village store and some attractive cottages, one bearing a 1639 datestone.

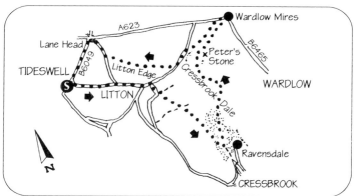

Head along the street, passing the school and the Clergy House, and turn right at a T-junction *(Cresswell & Monsal Dale)* out of the village just before the Methodist Church. At the first bend go left on a rough walled lane, and from a stile on the right a faint path heads down the field. At the bottom bear left, rising across two fields to a stile onto a grassy lane. Cross straight over and resume the slant, left, up through several fields.

Back down to the left are increasing views of Cressbrook Dale, with Peter's Stone particularly prominent higher up the valley: this will soon be far better seen. **From the top corner stile, bear left to a fence-stile into the trees atop Cressbrook Dale.** The lower part of Cressbrook Dale is also known as Ravensdale, and across the valley, part-hidden by trees, are gleaming limestone cliffs. These include Raven Buttress, hosting a wealth of popular climbs, while beneath, Ravencliffe Cave has yielded evidence of Ice Age occupation over 10,000 years ago.

The thin path heads away along the wood top before wooden steps signal a steep descent though the trees to join a broader path. Double back left on here through a clearing, staying out of the trees as it

swings down to the dale floor. Cross the plank bridge over the virtually dry floor to enter the Cressbrook Dale National Nature Reserve. Within a couple of minutes the path forks. Stay on the left one, a reserve path which runs a fine course up-dale to leave the trees behind. The dale opens out dramatically now, revealing steep flanks so typical of the White Peak's dry limestone dales.

Peter's Stone, Cressbrook Dale

The delightful path runs up the valley floor, passing one or two abandoned mineshafts and being joined by a path descending from the right. A stile beyond here offers a direct return to Litton up the little side valley of Tansley Dale, but our route forges on up-dale. The last stage curves round the narrowing valley, increasingly past modest limestone scars. **The highlight is passing beneath the tower-like outcrop of Peter's Stone.** It is the result of a landslip thousands of years ago, though its alternative name of Gibbet Rock tells another story: in 1812 it was the scene of the country's last gibbetting, when the body of a murderer (Anthony Lingard) hanged at Derby was brought here for public display. **The path becomes enclosed at the end to run out onto the A623 at Wardlow Mires.**

Just yards to the right at the road junction is a cosy little pub, the *Three Stags Heads*, and also a cafe across from it. **Our way goes left for a minute, then take a stile on the left. Rise away with the wall to a stile**

50

at the top, then cross to a corner stile. This section is dominated by the presence of Peter's Stone, now seen to better advantage below. **From the corner stile rise with the wall to a stile onto Mires Lane, and go left to the brow just short of Litton.** Again, enjoy superb views down into upper Cressbrook Dale. A choice awaits on the brow, a direct return through the village, or a more varied option.

The Red Lion, Litton

Just before the first house on the right, turn up a rough track to a gate and stile behind it. This runs up a field to a gateway at the top corner: pass through and climb the fieldside to a stile. The way is now straightforward, running a fairly straight line just set back from the modest Litton Edge with several glimpses down over the village.

Reaching a stile with a gate alongside, there is no sight of the next stile ahead. Rise to the brow and Tideswell appears down to the left: bear right for the house at Bank Farm, down in the far corner of the field. A stile just short of the corner admits onto Conjoint Lane. Go right towards the junction at Lane Head with a pub, the *Anchor*, across the road, and turn left on the footway down the B6049 for a long half-mile into Tideswell.

11

MONK'S DALE

START *Miller's Dale*   *Grid ref. SK 138732*

DISTANCE *6 miles*

ORDNANCE SURVEY MAPS
1:50,000
Landranger 119 - Buxton, Matlock & Dove Dale
1:25,000
Outdoor Leisure 24 - Peak District, White Peak

ACCESS *Start from the National Park's Miller's Dale (Monsal Trail) car park at the old station off the B6049. Served by Tideswell-Buxton buses (mostly from Sheffield) and Sunday/BH Monday buses from Castleton to Buxton.*

A magnificent ramble based on the Wye, but dominated by the return through two stunning side valleys: the village of Wormhill is worth the walk in itself. Allow ample time for the last mile and half, you can't, and shouldn't, rush through the likes of Monk's Dale.

S Miller's Dale was one of the largest stations on the Midland Railway's London-Manchester line, and featured a branch to Buxton. Opened in 1863, it was extended 40 years later and a second viaduct added. The major platforms survive but most impressive feature is the pair of mighty viaducts high above the valley: the walk concludes by crossing one of them. The station buildings house a ranger base, information boards and toilets. There is a popular tearoom opposite the car park. Our walk starts and ends on the Monsal Trail which now takes advantage of the old railway. See WALK 19 for more on the trail.

From the old station gain the Monsal Trail and turn right (west) bound for Chee Dale and Buxton. At the end of the platforms the trail chugs on into woodland. An early feature is the former East Buxton

limekilns. The two mighty kilns operated from 1880 to 1944 to supply quicklime for agriculture and the chemical industry. The concrete buttresses were added in the 1920s. A path slants up to the top to find a surviving jubilee waggon on rusting rails. Behind is the vast quarry itself. The side tipping waggons loaded the kilns with the necessary lime and coal: each was brought on narrow gauge tracks, as the latter came to the sidings below to be hauled up the slope by cable.

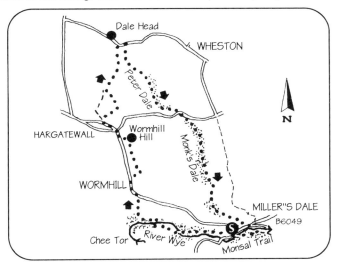

Just past here the line is carried by a viaduct over the river Wye. Yards further a blocked tunnel entrance bars the way. A footpath crosses the line here however, so from a stile on the right drop to another and on the path across the contrastingly open green pasture to slant down to the river. En route we pass beneath spoil heaps from the excavated tunnel. Arrival at the river is a grand moment, linger here by the Wye's clear flowing waters.

From the footbridge crossroads take the path rising up the bank, over a limestone floor and through scrubby undergrowth. During this pleasurable slant some fine views over the dale can be enjoyed. **At the top it runs up through a meadow, above a little side valley then becomes enclosed to rise to a cottage and road on the edge of Wormhill.**

Go left up the road to reach the green. En route we have a glimpse of Wormhill Hall over to the right, while on the left Wellhead Farm offers an extensive range of refreshments. The village green sports a set of stocks and a monument to James Brindley (1716-1772) in the form of a well spilling into three troughs. Born within this parish at neighbouring Tunstead, he went on to become one of the great civil engineers. His Bridgwater Canal of 1761 ushered in the canal era and indeed he became known as the father of the English canal system.

Turn down the lane to St. Margaret's church, all but hidden on the right. This enchanting spot could be anywhere and almost any time in rural England. In the secretively enclosed churchyard wild flowers thrive in unchecked grass and the birds sing without restraint. Though largely the result of Victorian restoration, the base of the tower dates back more than 700 years, with a highly individual roof added in more recent times: as I watched, a jackdaw slipped in to bring food to its squawking young. A cross stands in a base with a tiny sundial on top.

Past the church the lane becomes rough: just after the cottage on the left a path heads off the lane, briefly zigzagging and enclosed before heading along to the left through a series of gap-stiles along the backs of farm buildings. Crossing a green lane continue up the field-sides to arrive at a corner at the hamlet at Wormhill Hill. From the gate alongside the first house join the access road and follow this left, out onto the road. Turn right (gleaning the first open views from this footway) to a crossroads, and straight over on the lesser road ahead for the hamlet of Hargatewall.

This descends past a large Victorian house with a stable block to a minor dip. Fork right here on the lesser road, passing the attractive Hargate Hall on the right. After the cottages behind, turn down a drive to the right (opposite a black & white house), running down past the backs of the houses and into a field. When the track fades in the next field bear left to a stile in the very far corner. Now go left through several wall-corner stiles into an open field.

Slant right, down to a stile midway and across to join a descending track. Going down through one gate it ends at a stile below. Continue down the other side of the wall to a low stile at the bottom, with Peter Dale now just beneath. Go left across the field to the head of an old green way, which leads down onto the narrow road at Dale Head.

Go right past the cottage and take a stile on the right. While Hay Dale goes off to the left (see WALK 7), our way heads along the dry floor of Peter Dale. Increasingly colourful country is entered as the path runs along the dale floor, with limestone walls and natural rock gardens. A brief opening out is followed by a similarly brief enclosed section before running on to the road at the head of Monk's Dale.

Jubilee waggon,
East Buxton kilns,
Miller's Dale

Crossing straight over, Monk's Dale is entered. The path hurries us on to enter a dark ravine with steep walls and dense, dank foliage. This is an important remnant of semi-natural woodland, designated a National Nature Reserve and managed by English Nature. **Here we commence a full mile's section that is quite beyond compare with anything else in the book. The path squirms through the dale floor in the midst of dense undergrowth that resembles a sub-tropical habitat: no wonder it is so enthusiastically protected.**

Eventually, after an intervening stile, the path escapes up to the left to run along the base of the open bank. It drops quickly down with an old wall but not back into the undergrowth. Indeed the undergrowth largely falls away as we resume virtually on the dale floor but now not claustrophobic. Outstanding walking continues down to a waymark sending us a little up the slope to run atop a modest scar. This little effort is repaid with fine views back up-dale. The path slants back down to the floor and continues down again, past a marsh marigold pool to reach a largely superfluous footbridge.

The path leads briefly down the other side, rising a little to a brow to leave the reserve. Drop down to the gate below, from where a flight of steps leads down to the church in Miller's Dale. St. Anne's (1880) slots neatly into the limited space available in this pokey corner. **Cross the B6049 to the side road to Litton Mill.** On the right here is an old iron waterwheel still in situ, with the *Angler's Rest* pub just yards further.

Between waterwheel and pub a path breaks off to cross the Wye on a footbridge before climbing to join the Monsal Trail at some old kilns. These massive specimens of the Miller's Dale limeworks operated from 1878 to 1930 to provide quicklime for industry and agriculture (sweetening land). Featured are four great arches, themselves dwarfed by the whole structure (illustrated on page 47). Charged with crushed limestone and coal, this was burned in the kilns to produce quicklime which was then taken away by rail. A concession path offers a detour of less than a mile to visit the old quarry on the hillside above, and is described in WALK 9. A leaflet *Miller's Dale Quarry Nature Reserve* can usually be obtained at National Park Centres. **Turn right for two minutes back on the Monsal Trail, concluding over Miller's Dale Viaduct, alarmingly high above river and road!**

St. Margaret's Wormhill

12

CHEE DALE

START *Wye Dale*   *Grid ref. SK 104724*

DISTANCE *7½ miles*

ORDNANCE SURVEY MAPS
1:50,000
Landranger 119 - Buxton, Matlock & Dove Dale
1:25,000
Outdoor Leisure 24 - Peak District, White Peak

ACCESS *Start from the National Park's Wye Dale car park on the A6, opposite Topley Pike Quarry. Served by Buxton-Chesterfield (via Tideswell) and Summer Sunday/BH Monday Buxton-Bakewell buses.*

A wealth of natural and historic features pave the way for an stunningly beautiful walk with the Wye through Chee Dale.

NOTE: When the river is high the path through Chee Dale can become impassable, even before reaching the celebrated stepping stones (in normal conditions the stones themselves are sound enough). An alternative finish involves paths to the north via Hassop Farm, Flag Dale and Meadow.

S **From the car park cross the road to an uninspiring start at the quarry entrance. A path runs alongside the access road, then on beyond the immediate workings and into trees. Within five minutes this gruesome sight is behind us, and the contrastingly appealing green dry valley of Marl Dale opens up. Beyond the perimeter fence a guidepost indicates a fork. Go straight on up the short-lived dry valley in front, hemmed in by limestone cliffs. This quickly ends at dark craggy walls at Churn Holes. The path cleverly spirals up (pause to look back in horror at the quarry) above a cave to escape into lush limestone pastures.**

Head away up the field-side, and when the wall turns away keep straight on to meet a farm track. In this large pasture the map identifies a settlement, and sure enough if you stand and look around you can easily discern the low banks and walls of a network of small enclosures of ancient, probably Celtic origin. **Cross over the track to a stile in the corner ahead, and advance through several fields to pass by Burrs Farm. Continue rising to a green walled way ahead, and rise above it to quickly become more securely enclosed by walls, a rough lane forming to lead out onto the A5270.**

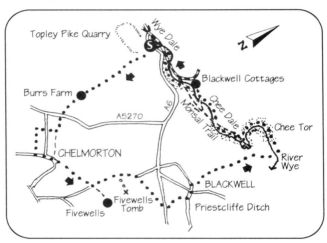

Just in front is Chelmorton nestling beneath the rounded knoll of Chelmorton Low up to our left. **Cross straight over and along a farm road leading through to the village. More interestingly, turn off this at the first chance by an old green walled way down to the right. Cross straight over a narrow road and down a similar way. Leave this at a stile on the left towards the end. Head along the slender field and one beyond it to emerge onto the main street by way of a garden.**

Turn left along the street to a junction, then up the lane between pub and church. Chelmorton is a peaceful, unassuming street village, and appropriately sited at its head are both church and pub. St. John the Baptist's boasts a tall spire, while the suitably named *Church Inn* dispenses well kept ales and a happy atmosphere.

Here the road ends. Take the main path winding up above the churchyard. Immediately on the left is a stile accessing a spring, once the villagers' water supply. **Continue up this track, soon easing out and running through a broad section of rough terrain on the line of a mineral vein to emerge onto a roadhead. With Fivewells Farms ahead, turn left on the more inviting old lane rising to a brow. Just below, it drops to Pillwell Gate.**

Fivewells Cairn

At this point, before continuing, a stile and sign on the right invite a detour on a concession path to Fivewells Chambered Tomb. The tomb itself can be discerned just five minutes away on the skyline to the east. The path runs across the first field then along the right-hand wall-side to a gap-stile just short of the tomb. This is a fine specimen of a burial site from Neolithic times (maybe 5000 years old!). The remaining stones reveal the 'back to back' arrangement of two chambers, now open to the skies, with their portal stones at the entrances still proudly in place. 19th century excavations revealed a number of skeletons. Surrounded by a kerbed embankment it occupies an exposed location on this distinct knoll, indeed it is said to be the highest such site in Britain. It is named, like the farm, after the 'Five Wells' shown on the map in a hollow nearby (no access).

Back on the main route, turn through the gate and down to the entrance to the former Calton Hill quarry site on the left. Turn right along the road, but forge straight on a grassy lane slanting down to

meet the A6. If desperate, the *Waterloo* pub is just up to the right. **The route crosses straight over to a stile and down the field-side outside the trees. Approaching Blackwell, the way swings right in the bottom field, with a groove, to a stile out onto a road at Priestcliffe Ditch. Turn down to a crossroads with the B6049 and straight over for the hamlet of Blackwell. Take the drive on the right for Blackwell Hall, there rising left towards the large farm complex. Pass to its right on a concrete road to emerge into the fields.**

Remain on the track straight ahead, ignoring turnings right then left before the track turns to abruptly end in a field. Turn down the wall-side to a stile across the bottom. Here we enter a limestone pasture to be greeted by a sudden and impressive prospect looking up Chee Dale. This is a superb moment as the steep walled valley floor runs away to the left, cradling the final delectable leg of our walk. **Advance on through a crumbling wall.** Here we pass alongside a less discernible ancient field system at the back of the prow of Chee Tor. **At the brow a steep descent commences to the river Wye.** En route we pass above a tunnel on the former railway, with excavated spoil still heaped above.

Cross the footbridge on the river and turn upstream through immediately lovely surrounds. A continuous set of weirs are in place to ensure suitable conditions for the spawning salmon, by way of forming pools in times of low water, and also helping aereate the water. **The splendour improves throughout the next long section into the wonders of Chee Dale. The path runs over rock steps and works its way past the delightful gurgle of Wormhill Springs to enter the heart of the limestone gorge.** At the bend the tall wall of Chee Tor reaches skyward on the left, a hugely popular climbing area featuring over 80 expert routes, while just ahead, the similarly popular Cornice lurks above our path. If the water level should be high then we might already have encountered an impasse.

The crunch comes on reaching the much vaunted stepping stones. In normal conditions they provide an absorbing traverse through the gorge, with the limestone wall there for a steadying hand throughout. If the river is high, then 'interesting' is not the word. I have watched people remove their boots and wade, yet I retained mine and stayed dry, just: it all depends on that water level! **Beyond here the river is crossed by a footbridge beneath the impressive viaduct.** Here we are in Derbyshire Wildlife Trust's Chee Dale Nature Reserve.

Just beyond, a branch path climbs to gain the Monsal Trail, but is **inferior to the riverside path which drops back down to another footbridge.** Note the contrast of the gorge downstream with the sedate glidings upstream. **Continuing, more stunning moments are enjoyed.** These include a set of far sturdier stepping stones: if you managed the first then you'll sail through these. **At the next viaduct there is another chance to rise onto the Monsal Trail. This is an option worth considering as it offers broader views, passing a junction with another viaduct before forging on to the end of the Trail.**

The river path however continues on, passing beneath that other viaduct (footbridge and further chance to join the Trail) before continuing upstream to Blackwell Cottages. High above to the left, incidentally, we have passed beneath the celebrated Plum Buttress, which offers the Peak's longest vertical climbing route. Now long gone, Blackwell Mill stood within a triangle of railway lines, one of which remains to serve one of Europe's largest quarries as it eats into the hillside opposite. The cottages once housed railway workers, for Blackwell Halt was one of the country's smallest stations, its platforms just one carriage length. A stone hut often purveys refreshments.

Cross the footbridge and head off on the drive, upstream beneath a viaduct at the terminus of the Trail. Simply continue upstream on this drive, under two final viaducts to return to the car park.

Plum Buttress,
Chee Dale

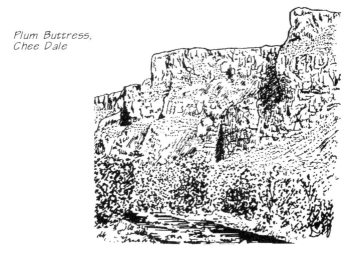

13

FIVE DALES

START *Wye Dale*   *Grid ref. SK 104724*

DISTANCE *6½ (or 5½) miles*

ORDNANCE SURVEY MAPS
1:50,000
Landranger 119 - Buxton, Matlock & Dove Dale
1:25,000
Outdoor Leisure 24 - Peak District, White Peak

ACCESS *Start from the National Park's Wye Dale car park on the A6, opposite Topley Pike Quarry: Served by Buxton-Chesterfield buses and Summer Sunday/BH Monday Buxton-Bakewell buses.*

Largely gentle walking through dry, green valleys. Springtime is strongly recommended.

S **From the car park cross the road to an uninspiring start at the quarry entrance. A path runs alongside the access road, then on beyond the immediate workings and into trees. Within five minutes this gruesome sight is behind us, and the contrastingly appealing green valley of Marl Dale opens up. Beyond the perimeter fence a guidepost indicates a fork.**

Take the branch right, which climbs the nab end then bears right outside the quarry fence. Quickly a stony track forms to run on past the quarry lagoon and deposit us into poor Deep Dale proper. A contrastingly thin but clear path heads away through undergrowth that seems not to have seen a grazing sheep for many a long year. Through scrub and occasional scree the path runs on this sinuous dry valley to reach a path crossroads beneath a small cave in the knob of rock up to our left. The path right is a quick escape out of the valley for King Sterndale.

Resuming from the crossroads, two further minutes see us reach Thurst House Cave. Excavations in the late 19th century revealed the bones of countless animals, confirming it was occupied by hunter-cave dwellers thousands of years ago. It has a vast gaping entrance which with a torch can be penetrated some distance. It also makes a fine vantage point for the next stage, up through the deepest cragbound confines of the dale with Raven's Tor high to the right.

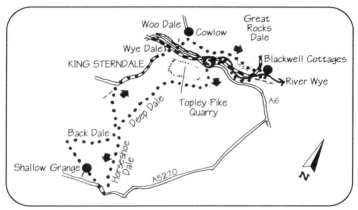

The improving path emerges at a stile into a clearing, where the dales fork into Horseshoe and Back Dales, each taking a path with them. We shall return down the latter, but for now take a well-earned easy ramble up the left arm, Horseshoe Dale. Here we join the Priests Way, an historic route to a monastic grange at King Sterndale. **This is a contrastingly genteel stroll along a delectable green valley, emerging unfailingly via farm buildings at the top onto the A5270.**

Go right along the verge for a few minutes as far as a stile, and make for the field's far corner. From the stile cross to the drive in front of Shallow Grange Farm, straight over it to a gate and stile past the garden wall. Go right on another drive to the end of the buildings. The track turns along the back into a caravan site, but keep straight on to the corner, with a stile just yards to the left. Cross the large field to the opposite wall, and go right to find a stile 50 yards short of a gate. Over to the left, vast quarry workings high above Buxton are only a mile distant from us. **Descend to the far corner, where a stile overlooks a meeting of dry valleys on a smaller scale to the earlier one.**

Descend and turn right along the floor of Back Dale, leading rapidly back to the clearing at the head of Deep Dale. Just yards short of it take a bridle-gate on the left and a good path - the Priests Way again - zigzags up the bank. Turn right along the edge for a couple of minutes. This proves a superb vantage point over Deep Dale, looking down to the black hole of Thurst House Cave and beyond. Too quickly our way swings left with the wall to a bridle-gate. Head up the field to a gate at the top, from where a faint green track slants to the far corner to join a rough lane.

Go right on the lane to meet the cul-de-sac road to King Sterndale. Turn right on it for a good half-mile, very broad verges between walls. En route we pass between the church - Christ Church, of 1847, and the school which closed in the 1950s. Progressing, the hall is in its parkland on the left, and the knoll of Chelmorton Low on the right beyond the upper scars of Deep Dale. The road ends in the select hamlet.

Deep Dale from the Priests Way

Keep straight on the ensuing track, passing the restored market cross stump on the green and quickly delving into trees as little more than a footpath. Almost at one take a stile on the right, from where a thin path drops steeply to the railway line. This serves Tunstead Quarry, of which more to come. Beneath it the path runs down onto the A6. Go right a few yards and cross with care to a farm bridge on the Wye. Note that for a near instant finish, you can dabble with death by staying on the right to be back at the car park within a few minutes.

Our full route takes the green track heading away into the foot of Woo Dale. Almost at once however take a less obvious green way turning sharp right, winding steeply up the hillside to the top: the farm buildings of Cowdale are just up to the left. Go right to a corner stile and head away with the wall along the field top. Enjoy good views down well wooded Chee Dale to some fine limestone tors, even though the scene is immediately tempered by Topley Pike Quarry's appearance. **Keep on almost to the far end, where at the wall corner turn left with it up to a stile.** Whatever we think of large scale quarrying in National Parks, it's certainly interesting to see! (indeed, with further extensions refused, its closure is on the cards).

If the waymarker still points up the field from it, ignore it and turn right along the top side of the wall. This runs on to tapering walls and a stile into thin woodland. A suitably thin path runs along through the trees alongside an old wall. Towards the bottom take an obvious gateway in the old wall and a thin path heads off left into enthusiastic undergrowth. This lasts for only a minute before reaching a crumbling wall again, now in front. Step over and ensure you locate the path heading away. It drops gently down through a scrubby pasture with the bulk of the woodland on the right.

The path runs down to an old stile in a gap in the trees at the bottom to reveal a view of Great Rocks Dale. In front is another area of country devastated by former quarrying. Stretching a long mile or so away to the left however is the still very active Tunstead Quarry, served by the rail line immediately beneath us. This is one of Europe's largest quarries, and its vastness makes Topley Pike seem like a Legoland version. Contrast this with the view down the Wye, looking to the celebrated Plum Buttress, which offers the Peak's longest vertical climbing route; and with Blackwell Cottages, bridge, river and old railway line all just beneath us.

Turn right here, the path zigzagging cleverly down to bridge an old cutting and down to an underpass on the rail line. Faced with the Wye the path goes left past a red brick pump house to arrive at Blackwell Cottages. A stone hut often purveys refreshments. Long gone Blackwell Mill stood within a triangle of railway lines: the cottages once housed railway workers, for Blackwell Halt was one of the country's smallest stations, its platforms just one carriage length. **Cross the footbridge and head off along the drive, which runs upstream in the charming company of the wooded Wye, beneath several viaducts to return to the car park.**

CHELMORTON & FLAGG

START *Taddington*   *Grid ref. SK 142710*

DISTANCE *6½ miles*

ORDNANCE SURVEY MAPS
1:50,000
Landranger 119 - Buxton, Matlock & Dove Dale
1:25,000
Outdoor Leisure 24 - Peak District, White Peak

ACCESS *Start from the village centre. Ample parking, with care, on the long main street. Served by Buxton-Bakewell buses (Manchester-Nottingham express).*

An undemanding stroll through the fields, linking three less 'touristy' Peak villages, each with a pub to offer. Chelmorton is the highlight.

S   The street village of Taddington, long since by-passed by the A6, is watched over by the spired church of St Michael & All Angels. Though restored in 1891 it retains 14th century work in its tower, while in the spacious churchyard stands a thousand year old carved cross shaft 6ft in height. Also in evidence are the *Queens Arms* pub, a Primitive Methodist Church of 1903, an old white 'London' mile-stone, a shop, an 18th century hall, and a cafe on the main road.

From the church gate head west along the main street to the Flagg junction, named Humphrey Gate. At once a narrow snicket climbs away between houses into a field. Slant up through successive gap-stiles to join a road. From here there is a good view back over the village. **Cross straight over and on a thin path up the fields behind, through a labyrinth of crumbled walls. The faint way then slants left up a larger field, aiming for trees on the skyline. From the corner stile slant up the side of a covered reservoir at Sough Top.**

From the corner stile head away with the wall, the route now infallible as it simply remains with this wall. In amongst we pass several reminders of lead mining, most notably a covered shaft right by the path. Ahead are a range of modern limestone quarries outside the Park boundary above Buxton, while the rolling country down to the left secretes Flagg.

Meeting a green lane, cross straight over and resume as before, passing Fivewells Farms and crossing the last field to join a road. Go right a few yards then cross to a narrow strip of rough terrain on the line of a mineral vein. This leads directly down into Chelmorton. Towards the bottom it narrows and drops more steeply down to the head of the village, rather tidily between church and pub. Just short of the lanehead we pass a spring, once the villagers' water supply.

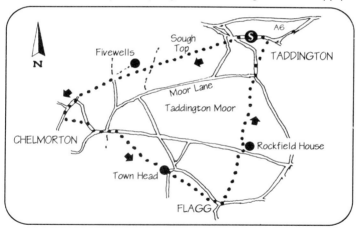

Chelmorton is a peaceful, unassuming street village, and appropriately sited at its head are both church and pub. St. John the Baptist's boasts a tall spire, while the suitably named *Church Inn* dispenses well kept ales and a happy atmosphere. A solid green booth along the street makes an individual phone kiosk.

At the junction just below, the direct way goes left along the road, but better to head down the main street and see something of the place. Half-way along, just after a footpath sign on the right, one on the left sends us into a wide open concrete yard. Pass through to a

gate at the top, then up the fieldside to a steep little pull to a stile onto the road (not as on earlier maps). At this point pause to look back over a fine prospect of the environs of Chelmorton village, revealing a fascinating arrangement of enclosures. Countless narrow strips run out from the backs of the dwellings: these remarkable wall patterns recall a long abandoned farming system when it appears almost every household lay claim to its own individual strip.

Go right on the road then left at the T-junction. Cross over the junction on the brow then one field further take a stile on the right. A trod slants down past a wall corner to a hidden stile in the very bottom corner, then bears left to stile part-way along. Maintain this angle through two further fields then swing round past High Stool farm buildings to successive stiles/gates onto a narrow lane. Almost opposite, another stile sends us off down a gentle hollow, through a number of intervening stiles with Flagg village forming on the left. In the last, longer field (the third after a pocket wood) bear left to a gap-stile onto the road.

Go right just as far as a junction. Here sits a tiny green outside the old village school and Methodist Church of 1883. The village pub, the *Plough*, is just a minute further along the street. **Turn left up the drive to Flagg Hall.** The hall itself is passed on the right, an attractive, substantial farmhouse. **Keep straight on between the buildings to emerge into a field. A track heads away but bear left to a stile ahead, passing through a small nature refuge comprising a pond and newly planted trees. From here head along the centre of a long field to emerge onto a road by a stile and gate at the far end.** Again, while crossing this field note the parallel field walls, notably on the left.

Go right a few yards on the road then take a stile on the left. A very thin, long pasture rises away (past Rockfield House), but before the end take a stile on the right. Slant away to the next stile then up to a corner gate, with another gate just beyond. Up again to a stile ahead, behind which is a crossroads of footpaths. Pass through the crumbling wall and up a faint hollow to the next stile, then swing right on an increasingly faint trod to the far corner of successive fields to emerge via a stile onto a road junction.

Go left along the main (Taddington) road. Known as the Jarnett, it offers sweeping views to the north. **Just over the brow take an inviting green way slipping down to the right between walls. Taddington is now just beneath us, and the limestone way runs pleasantly down, narrowing to debouch onto the main street alongside the village hall.**

15

LONGSTONE EDGE & FOOLOW

START Eyam   Grid ref. SK 217763

DISTANCE 8¾ miles

ORDNANCE SURVEY MAPS
1:50,000
Landranger 119 - Buxton, Matlock & Dove Dale
1:25,000
Outdoor Leisure 24 - Peak District, White Peak

ACCESS Start from the village centre. There is a car park just off the main street, west of the hall. Served by bus from Sheffield, Chesterfield and Buxton via Calver and Tideswell.

A real variety of scenery where limestone meets gritstone. Ever changing views and much of interest, including several villages. For more on Eyam itself, please refer to WALK 16.

❺   Leave the church by heading east on the main street (Church Street) to the small square. Known as the Bull Ring, an old ring remains in place from bull baiting days, now beneath a cover. **Cross right to a phone box marking the start of Lydgate.** This narrow road was the old main road into the village, still passable all the way to Stoney Middleton. On the right we pass the Lydgate Graves, two solitary gravestones in a small enclosure, still clearly legible reminders of the plague. **Head along to the lane end at a few houses.**

As the old road sneaks off left, take a stile straight ahead. Passing a couple of houses the track runs into a field. Head on to the end, where an enclosed footway takes over. Emerging onto the open pasture of the Cliff, a faint way runs on to a solitary rock. This is an original boundary stone from the plague days. Carved in the top are a number of holes where money would be left in payment for food and goods from the outside world for the beleaguered villagers. The holes would be filled with vinegar to disinfect the coins.

Continue on and down the broad end with Stoney Middleton ahead, on a nice path down to a stile onto the old road. Go right, dropping down to the main road at the first opportunity after passing the Methodist chapel. Cross straight over between the octagonal toll house (now a fish & chip shop) and the *Moon* pub.

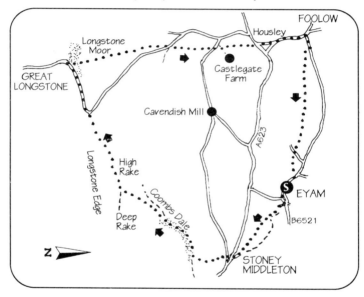

Stoney Middleton is a curious village, squashed tightly into a narrow gorge with cottages climbing each side. St. Martin's church was built by Joan Eyre in thanks for the return of her husband from the Battle of Agincourt. Only the tower remains from that time: the octagonal (again!) nave of 1759 is of particular interest. Above the village, the road runs up Middleton Dale, a deep, wooded gorge. Its tall limestone walls are divided between rock climbers and quarrymen, the latter having rendered much of the hillside to the south absolutely desolate.

Head straight up a footway up the other side to emerge by the school. Go up to the right a short way then left along Eaton Fold leading to Vicarage Lane. Immediately there is a fine view left across to Curbar and Baslow Edges across the Derwent Valley. **Keep straight on the drive to pass beneath a new house. Before the next house, take a gate on the left and along to a gate/stile into a field. Advance to the barn ahead and take a stile to its left. Here the path forks. Take the nearest stile in the fence to the right, and curve away on a faint, fading path descending into Coombs Dale. Slant down to locate a stile at the base of the bank, from where a few planks lead through undergrowth onto a narrow surfaced track.**

Turn right, up the dale floor. This curious route could accommodate a Mini for some distance, subject to not meeting anything else! It affords easy progress however while admiring the steep flanks and occasional limestone outcrops. **Turning a corner the dale opens out, and a broad track takes over. Immediately on crossing the hole dug to stop anyone driving through, go left to a stile in a fence. A green path heads away along a side valley. Within 20 yards turn up to the right, slanting back up above the main valley. Quickly a firmer path forms, and this well made trod traverses the steep flank.**

Below is Sallet Hole Mine, operating until recently. An arched and blocked mine entrance, source of the valley's tiny stream, is alongside the buildings. Recent landscaping has ensured that before too long the surroundings will mellow. **The path rises through a little rough heather to a stile out of the valley. Cross the field to stiles past a barn, and then cross a vast mineral rake.**

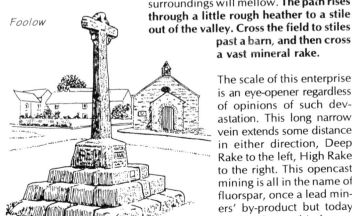

Foolow

The scale of this enterprise is an eye-opener regardless of opinions of such devastation. This long narrow vein extends some distance in either direction, Deep Rake to the left, High Rake to the right. This opencast mining is all in the name of fluorspar, once a lead miners' by-product but today used in the steel industry.

71

Across, turn right on the very broad track, which runs parallel to the rake. On the brow the view south opens out, revealing a wide prospect over Longstone Edge to the environs of Bakewell. **Simply remain on this track past abandoned workings, and gaining a little more height before dropping down to the bend of a minor road.** Longstone Moor is outspread ahead, with Fin Cop, site of an Iron Age hillfort, dropping into Monsal Dale to the left. **Turn left down the verges of this quiet road.** Savouring views over the Longstones, count several dewponds in the fields below our steep bank.

Beyond a cattle-grid a woodland corner is entered. Just round the bend, and the end of the trees, take a gate into Black Plantation and a clear path rises away. Crossing a green track it climbs through trees to a gate and stile onto Longstone Moor. A grand moment: the path continues straight up to the brow, revealing a sweeping prospect of heather moorland. Continue on, across an old mine track and, keeping left at a fork, rising to a guidepost on the final brow. Revealed ahead now are Abney Moor, Bradwell Moor, and through to the Mam Tor ridge and Kinder Scout. **The path descends towards a wall; ignore other turnings and head straight down to a stile off the moor.** Over to the left is Wardlow strung along its road.

Cross to a stile opposite and head along the field to the next, then cross to one onto a road. Go straight over to a small gate and the path resumes, slanting left, crossing an access track and the faint path holding this line across numerous fields aiming for prominent Castlegate Farm ahead, backed by trees. Another road is crossed, and a field corner cut to a stile onto the farm drive.

Cross straight over the farm drive also, to a stile, then cross to the far corner behind the trees. From a gap-stile between the gates advance to a stile ahead, then aim for the houses at Housley. A stile in the bottom corner lead on to Housley House, passing a dewpond keep left of its confines to a corner stile onto the A623. Cross straight over and along the road into Foolow. A footway soon appears to help us along.

Foolow is a gem of a village, off the main tourist path yet a real delight. Everything sits back from the green, which is decorated by a 14th century cross (moved to its present position in 1868) and a circular duckpond. Also upon it are the old village well and a Victorian postbox. At one end is the pub the *Bulls Head*; the Hall; the Manor

House; the simple 19th century church of St. Hugh, with its bellcote; and the Wesleyan Reform Chapel, built in 1866 as the Foolow Chapel and Sunday School. In late August the well dressing ceremony brings further charm to the green.

Leave by turning right along the Eyam road, and within a couple of minutes take a stile on the right. Cross to a gap-stile by a little barn ahead, where another path comes in, then head away along the wall-side on a near straight line bound for Eyam. Stiles are numerous and beyond description, but the route remains fairly clear throughout. Parallel up to the left is Eyam Edge, a well defined, colourful scarp. If the thermals are deemed suitable, there may well be gliders wheeling overhead from the club up on Abney Moor. Sat atop the edge is the hamlet of Bretton, while further along, at the base of the slope, is the prominent Black Hole Mine.

An early interruption is the crossing of unassuming little Linen Dale, past which the way slants up left and on through old walls. A series of upright squeezer stiles, typical of this locality, add interest after crossing a green lane, before the final pastures as Eyam appears from a minor brow. A narrow back road is joined by way of a narrow snicket between houses. Cross straight over another road and a longer snicket runs down to a small housing estate, going straight ahead to re-enter the main street between car park and church.

Eyam Hall

16

BRETTON CLOUGH

START *Eyam*   *Grid ref. SK 217763*

DISTANCE *4¾ miles*

ORDNANCE SURVEY MAPS
1:50,000
Landranger 119 - Buxton, Matlock & Dove Dale
1:25,000
Outdoor Leisure 24 - Peak District, White Peak

ACCESS *Start from the village centre. There is a car park just off the main street, west of the hall. Served by bus from Sheffield, Chesterfield and Buxton via Calver and Tideswell.*

A climb out of the plague village to discover a 'hidden' valley.

S Eyam is one of the most famous villages in the Peak, and though it has many appealing corners its pulling power is due to being the historic 'plague village'. The story of its residents' suffering and fortitude in 1665-1666, when Bubonic Plague decimated the populace by around 250 is an absorbing one almost without parallel. The disease was carried by fleas that fed on infected rats in ships bringing cloth from China to London. Ably lead by rector William Mompesson, the villagers maintained a remarkably courageous stance by staying put and not letting the disease spread to neighbouring villages.

Centrepiece for the story is St. Lawrence's church, which features Norman pillars and font and a Jacobean pulpit. A striking modern feature is the plague window, depicting characters from the disaster. In the churchyard is a beautifully carved 8th century Celtic cross and many fascinating tombstones: best known is that of Catherine Mompesson, wife of the rector and one of the plague's last victims. See also the splendid sundial of 1775 on the church wall.

Facing the stocks in the main street is Eyam Hall, a beautiful house dating from 1676. It has been in the hands of the Wright family for over 300 years and is open to the public, while Eyam Museum is also centrally placed. Several shops and pubs serve villagers' and visitors' needs, while a youth hostel perches on the hillside above. Plaques scattered all over the village relate Eyam's own poignant story as it unfolds, far more effectively than a book or video could ever do! During these two walks from Eyam you will encounter some of them, but to do justice a full exploration of the village is recommended.

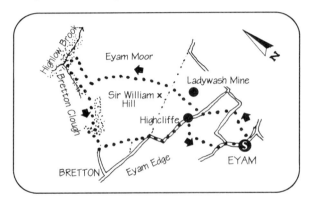

Leave the main street by a footpath up the inside of the churchyard. From a kissing-gate at the far end ignore other turnings and take the broad path rising directly away. Rising through scrub to a stile, continue up the field-side to a stile in a small wooded corner. Resume up the other side to a stile onto a road. Straight across a path climbs into woodland, initially a little roughly but then slanting across above the youth hostel. At the top Eyam Edge is gained. Look back for a fine view over the trees, beyond the village to the edges across and down the Derwent Valley: unfortunately, eyes are also drawn to the line of quarries flanking Middleton Dale.

From the corner stile a path runs left along the edge, and on through a further stile before being ushered away from the edge, crossing to the far corner of a field where a stile admits onto a road. Go left 25 yards to a stile on the right and head up the wall-side. On the left is a radio mast, on the right the chimney of the former Ladywash Mine, like so many other old lead workings re-opened over the years to abstract fluorspar. **With moorland waiting ahead, simply remain on the wall-side to reach a rough lane.** The white painted Ordnance Survey column on Sir William Hill (1407ft/429m) can be seen just up to the left. **Crossing straight over the joys of Eyam Moor are gained.**

A good path runs across the intensely heather moorland to a sturdy cairn on a modest edge. This marks a superb viewpoint, with the hauntingly beautiful Bretton Clough at our feet and Abney Moor beyond. Through the gap northwards are the Mam Tor ridge and Win Hill backed by Kinder Scout, while above Hathersage, Stanage Edge is arrayed. **Descend the path to reach the bottom corner of the moor, where three very different paths merge.**

Passing through the stile another classic moment is gained as a supreme green track curves down above a modest gritstone edge. This offers itself as an unparalleled viewpoint for Bretton Clough. The path curves round and turns down the valley. Beyond an intervening wall stay with that on the right to the ruins over the wall. Here our briefly fainter path drops down to the left, re-forming on entering bracken to double back down the bank to Stoke Ford. This is marked by an incongruous modern footbridge and an historic guidepost (illustrated on page 18). No less than five paths meet at this once important ford, which survives despite the footbridge. This peaceful setting at the confluence of the Bretton and Abney brooks is a hugely colourful scene and, again, a place to linger.

Our route however takes up with the main path met just above the bridge, and turns upstream on it. Always above the brook, it passes through that wall again then soon curves in to a side brook. Across, turn up the bank to the remains of Gotherage Barn. Here a broad green track drops down to a gateway, from where a faint way heads across a couple of fields. Towards the end the path is suddenly clear (not as on map) as it runs beneath a wooded bank. Approaching a clough the path turns up to soon cross it via a stile in the fence. Just beyond, it turns upstream to zigzag up to a seat on a knoll.

Heading away from the seat the path reaches a stile, then away with the wall rising to another stile and the start of a rough lane up onto a road. The *Barrel Inn* and youth hostel at Bretton are just five minutes along to the right. The pub is the highest in Derbyshire, though is overtopped by several Staffordshire pubs within the Peak. **Our way goes left, the road ending immediately at a lone house and a rough**

lane taking over. **Final views down into the clough are enjoyed before the lane runs on to join a road. Go left here, swinging right and then left as it starts to slant down the edge.** Outward views now return, featuring Eyam, some fine woodland on the slopes above it, and those quarries again.

Beyond a bend at a scattering of houses at Highcliffe, look out for a secretive way slipping down to the right. Descending this enclosed old way, quickly leave it at a footpath signed through a stile on the right. A thin path contours across to Jumber Brook and into woodland. It descends through the trees, under which is a dense springtime carpet of bluebells. At the bottom the path runs down an old wallside alongside minor evidences of mining.

The grassy old mine track merges in and down another field-side. At the bottom go right, round to the drive of the house, but then left on a short narrow way along the front. At the stile here, note the topstone rife with fossils. **The last field is a scruffy one, dropping to a gate into the top of the farmyard. Descend through here and down onto the road in the village. Turn left to finish.**

*Bretton
Clough*

17

MONSAL DALE & MILLER'S DALE

START *Monsal Head*   *Grid ref. SK 185715*

DISTANCE *7¼ miles*

ORDNANCE SURVEY MAPS
1:50,000
Landranger 119 - Buxton, Matlock & Dove Dale
1:25,000
Outdoor Leisure 24 - Peak District, White Peak

ACCESS *Start from the large public car park alongside the Monsal Head Hotel on the B6465. Served by Bakewell-Tideswell buses.*

Attractive limestone country divides two stunningly beautiful sections of the Wye, the opening mile through Monsal Dale and the classic two mile section from Litton Mill to the end.

S Monsal Head is a popular spot for walkers and tourists alike, for it offers outstanding views for no effort down onto a sharp bend of the Wye. A view indicator is found in the smaller car park, featuring the Monsal Viaduct dividing our start down Monsal Dale, to the left, and our conclusion through Upperdale on the right. The *Monsal Head Hotel* has all day opening, with a wide range of beers, gifts and crafts, and a cafe alongside.

Take the first stile at the top of the steep side road dropping away behind the cafe, and head along to the left on the lower path running on into the trees. This passes high above the viaduct, which will itself form the final steps of the walk. For now our path runs on through trees then descends to meet the Wye alongside a tumbling weir beneath a pond.

78

Just downstream a footbridge takes us over the river. Joining the path on the opposite side, resume downstream. This section alone is worth the entire walk's effort, a stunningly beautiful stretch of the Wye. Part wooded banks rise high above, notably on Fin Cop opposite. **Just short of the A6 a path junction is reached: take the main one left, down to a stile and along to join the main road at Lees Bottom. Cross with care to White Lodge car park and pass through it to a stile ahead, where a path heads away.**

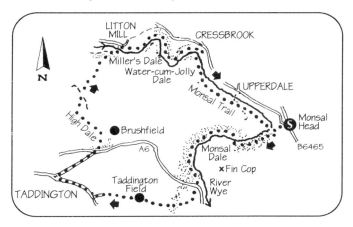

Shortly after the next stile a fork is reached: take the lesser branch right, rising through attractive limestone pasture above the head of a small ravine. Rising up this dry side valley, cross to the other side of a fence at a stile as the foliage becomes denser. At the top cross a field to Taddington Field Farm. At the end of the buildings a stile accesses the drive, which rises to a junction at Lodley View Farm. Over the brow, cut a corner by slipping down a leafy way to rejoin the road. Resume on here to Town End on the edge of Taddington.

If seeking refreshment the *Queens Arms* is handily sited just ahead: see WALK 14 for more on Taddington. **If not exploring, double back right down the road. This was the A6 until the village was mercifully by-passed. At the junction with the modern highway (at this point a dual carriageway) cross straight over to a green track rising away. It curves up to a brow and a gateway into a field, with Middle Farm, Brushfield ahead. Don't enter the field but turn up to a walled green way heading away. This soon drops down into High Dale.**

Go left along the dry valley floor, and when the wall parts company do likewise, a path slanting up a hollow on the right. Keep on through old walls to a stile at the top onto a green lane. Go left a short way to a stile on the right, then up the field-side away from a dewpond. A stile in the top corner accesses another path. Go right here amid mounds and hollows of old mine workings. Good views northwards extend beyond Abney Moor to the Mam Tor ridge and Kinder Scout.

The path goes left past a wall corner and down to a stile. Outspread is the deep trough of the Wye in Miller's Dale, with Tideswell Dale climbing away. Descend the wall-side, now in Derbyshire Wildlife Trust's Priestcliffe Lees nature reserve. The path descends through limestone and scrub pasture, at the bottom reaching a bridge on the Monsal Trail. Descend to the old line, but within yards forsake it as a path drops down through trees to Litton Mill. The line itself enters a sealed tunnel to the right. For more on the Monsal Trail, see page 89.

Litton Mill hamlet is entered by way of a footbridge over the river and millcut. Turn right to a 'square' where phone box and cafe stand. The mill began as a water powered cotton spinning mill in 1782, and is best known, unfortunately, for the appalling conditions of child labour that prevailed under its owner Ellis Needham. It remained in operation until recent times, but in 1996 the old mill stood as a terrible eyesore: plans for conversion to a holiday centre were faced by local opposition to a major scheme in a fragile location.

Just along the road rising away is the odd Chimney Cottage. Don't follow the road away, but head on past the mill on a concession footpath. This is courtesy of the landowners, Cressbrook & Litton Flyfishers Club, so be good! At the end it crosses the millcut and heads downstream between river and cut. A splendid path quickly takes shape through to the beginnings of Water-cum-Jolly Dale.

The cut rejoins us and an Arcadian walk ensues through this glorious dale, increasingly with impressive limestone walls above. The river in times of high water overflows lower down to create idyllic pools and wildlife ponds. Up above is a glimpse of old railway in a section between two tunnels, and the popular climbing ground known as the Cornice. By this time a true millpond features, constructed to provide extra water for Cressbrook Mill. Cliffs at our side shadow the water's edge, culminating in the awesome overhang of Rubicon Wall, a limestone classic featuring some of the hardest recorded climbs. The glories end at a works yard: cross the footbridge over a weir. Pause to look across the water to the crags, and downstream into a narrow, powerful gorge. **Climbing away the path rises left above Cressbrook Mill, on a track that runs on to rejoin the old railway at a tunnel entrance.** From here look back to view the setting of Cressbrook Mill.

Cressbrook began in 1783, like Litton a water powered cotton spinning mill, one of many established by Richard Arkwright. The original mill was soon destroyed by fire and replaced by what became known as the Old Mill. In 1815 the imposing 'Big Mill' was completed. A bell - still seen in the cupola - summoned workers, mostly child labourers from the cities. A row of cottages called Apprentices' Row housed the children. After a century of water power, steam turbines took over, and it was not until 1965 that manufacturing ceased.

Monsal Dale and Fin Cop

The final mile traces the Monsal Trail along to the viaduct at the start, passing the platform of Monsal Dale station. A simple hut affords shelter at a once animated scene where lead mining, limestone quarrying, livestock and indeed ramblers all made use of the railway. At this point the *Monsal Head Hotel* appears on the skyline ahead. Just beyond, a blocked mine entrance is followed by a bridged cutting. **A final pause on the viaduct reveals a lovely view down the walk's first mile.** Monsal Dale Viaduct itself is some 80ft high, and now acts as a symbol of the trail, frequently guesting on souvenirs of all types as a famous landmark of the Peak. **Across it a path spirals up through trees to emerge back at the start, and a welcome pint or cuppa.**

18

MAGPIE MINE

START *Ashford in the Water*   *Grid ref. SK 194696*

DISTANCE *6 miles*

ORDNANCE SURVEY MAPS
1:50,000
Landranger 119 - Buxton, Matlock & Dove Dale
1:25,000
Outdoor Leisure 24 - Peak District, White Peak

ACCESS *Start from the village centre. Small car park around the back from the church. Served by bus from Bakewell, Tideswell, Buxton and more distant express routes (Manchester, Nottingham, Sheffield).*

A grand walk by river and woodland, to find a delightful dry valley and a remarkable mining site.

S Ashford in the Water is a popular village, best known for its 17th century Sheepwash Bridge (see page 88) which served the thriving packhorse trade. Alongside is the pound where sheep were held for dipping, to wash their fleeces prior to clipping: an annual ceremony re-enacts this once workaday event. Ashford was a major fording point on the river Wye, back to at least Iron Age times when the important White Peak road the Portway came this way, later probably used by the Romans. There have been numerous small mills here over the centuries. Holy Trinity church was restored in 1870, but the tower survives from the 13th century. There are two pubs, the *Bulls Head* and the larger *Ashford Hotel*, and a Post office/shop/teashop.

From the parish church cross the road to the pump shelter (now minus its pump) and cross Sheepwash Bridge behind it. Over the main road, turn right on the footway for a few minutes then escape left along the side road to Sheldon. Again within minutes, as the road

**turns to begin its climb up Kirk Dale, a path turns off to the right after
a weir. Entering a riverside pasture, turn upstream on a clear path.**
We shall return on the green path slanting up from the river. The Wye
is in typical mood here as it glides effortlessly through delightful
surrounds, and the sudden flight of a heron is always likely. High
ahead is the big wooded bowl of Great Shacklow Wood.

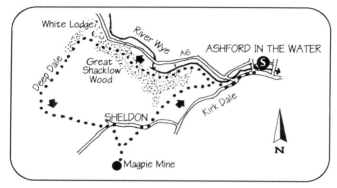

**Delightful walking leads to a bridge and an old sawmill under Great
Shacklow Wood.** This old watermill comprises two small buildings
and boasts two rusting iron wheels, attached to each side of the old
mill building: bobbins for the cotton mills were made here. A third
smaller wheel helped pump water to the farms at Sheldon, several
hundred feet above. **The path passes around the back and following
the former mill race quickly reaches Magpie Sough.** Here a great
stream of water emerges from a stone arch to run a mere few yards into
the river. This is the outflow of a 3-mile sough from the Magpie Mine,
made in 1873 to drain excess water away from the mining operation.

**Resuming, we part company from the river at some ponds, and the
path climbs the bottom of the wood before rising further into it. A
smashing woodland walk culminates in a sustained descent back out
at the far end. A junction with a bridleway is reached in open scrub
country. Go left, the fine green path contouring round to enter the
equally green floor of Deep Dale beneath a limestone knoll.**

**Simply head up the dry valley for virtually a mile between steep
enclosing flanks. Passing the remains of mine workings over the wall,
the valley begins to open out. Within a hundred yards of crossing the**

wall at a bridle-gate, re-cross by a stile and take the steep path climbing left to the skyline. A different scene is entered as Deep Dale is replaced by wide open country criss-crossed by drystone walls. **Bear left to the far corner gate.** By now the silhouette of the chimney and engine house at Magpie Mine should be seen over to the right.

Remain with the wall through several fields, all linked by gates. Note the stature of the adjacent wall, over 6ft high at times. **When the wall turns away, bear left to a stile with another one just behind it. Cross the length of the field to a stile by a gate onto the road just short of Sheldon: alongside is the tiniest of dewponds. Go left to the edge of the village. Here stands an informal green with houses set back.**

Magpie Mine

One could head straight on through the village but would miss Magpie Mine, so, take a gap-stile by a gate at the first house on the right. A little path runs through a little enclosure, and emerging, the mine is seen straight ahead. Bear left to a stile in the far corner, and round the wall corner just ahead, dropping down to a gap by a filled in gateway (not quite as per map). Cross to a stile in front then a path bears right across to another, to which we shall return. For now aim straight for the mine, one last stile giving access to the site.

The Magpie Mine is a magnificent example of a Cornish-type beam engine house, as anyone who has walked the Cornwall coast path will testify. With a main shaft 600ft deep, the mine closed as recently as 1958. Its happy state of preservation owes much to the efforts of the Peak District Mines Historical Society and the Peak National Park, for sufficient remains to gain an appreciation of the scale of things. Principal features are the engine house itself and the main chimney standing equally proud alongside. Nearby are many other features such as a steel winding drum and other winches, and another smaller, square chimney. A guidebook can be purchased from the nearby cottage (when open), originally the mine agent's house.

Leaving by the corner stile, return down the field to the previous one, then turn right down the wall-side. From the corner stile cross to one opposite with another behind, then a path heads away with the wall. This is sensibly diverted to emerge onto a road, this time at the other end of the village. Up to the left in the centre of this former mining community is a pub, the *Cock & Pullet*, and the simple St. Michael & All Angels' church, with a bell-cote and what from the outside appears to be all roof and nothing else.

Turn right down the road to Lower Farm in a hollow. After it take a stile on the left and the path heads away towards the top of Little Shacklow Wood. Within 50 yards, however, fork right on a lesser path contouring across to a stile. Behind it a level green way heads off, no doubt once a miners' track (from Ashford). This runs a grand course, curving above the wood-edge and dropping gently down outside it. Ahead are super views over the lower valley of the Wye.

From the wood corner at the end the way slants off, fading just beyond the end of an old wall. Keep straight on, and though the map suggests a bee-line straight ahead, the old track wisely avoids a potential scar on the end, and zigzags down to the left to rejoin the riverbank. Retrace steps back to the village.

Shacklow Mill

19

MONSAL TRAIL

START *Bakewell*   *Grid ref. SK 222689*

DISTANCE *7¾ miles*

ORDNANCE SURVEY MAPS
1:50,000
Landranger 119 - Buxton, Matlock & Dove Dale
1:25,000
Outdoor Leisure 24 - Peak District, White Peak

ACCESS *Start from the National Park's Monsal Trail car park at Bakewell station, above the town to the east. Served by bus from most places, with regular services from Tideswell, Matlock, Buxton, Manchester and Sheffield. Alternatively, start from the bridge in the town centre, in which case simply head upstream on the east bank to quickly pick up the route. Car parks nearby.*

Easy walking with a perfect centrefold at Monsal Head. Two attractive villages add further interest and the return is a preserved rail trail.

S Bakewell is featured at the start of WALK 20. **From the car park return along Station Road and down towards town, but take the first right along Burre Close, right along Castle Drive, then left on Castle Mount Crescent. This winds round to emerge onto the main road. Cross to steps descending to the river Wye in glorious surrounds, and turn upstream. The path quickly strikes off to join a back road. Go left on here to its terminus at Holme Bridge.**

This superb, narrow packhorse bridge dates from 1664, and with four low, main arches it feels almost miniature in character. Cross it to see the restored sheepwash, where fleeces were washed prior to clipping. Alongside is a millcut which supplied water from the Wye to a cornmill downstream.

Continue upstream on the private drive leading to the yard of Lumbford Mill. The original mill was built by Richard Arkwright in 1778 for spinning cotton. Today the site has a variety of uses. **Bear left of the buildings to join the main road. Go right on the footway, and leave at a gap-stile by a gate after the factory and just before houses. A path crosses the field, interrupted by snickets either side of a suburban street before resuming across the fields.** Down to the right, Mill Pond and Ashford Lake send foaming waterfalls over stepped weirs. Now attractive wildlife habitats, these were built to power waterwheels at Arkwright's mill: the upper pond was made in 1852 when greater power was needed to supply larger wheels.

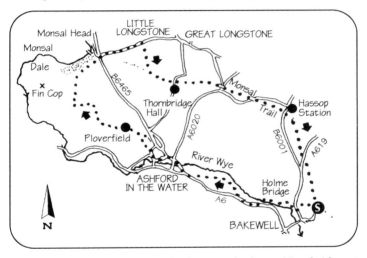

A delightful riverside pasture leads towards the waiting bridge at Ashford. The path bears left to join the road, then go immediately along the old road over the original graceful bridge. After crossing the river it bridges a millcut, which immediately downstream splits into two itself. **At the end cross the road and head along the village street.** Ashford in the Water is featured at the start of WALK 18. **From the church go right along the street to the pump shelter (minus its pump) in front of Sheepwash Bridge. Here turn right along Fennel Street, and at the crossroads with its slate canopied wooden memorial seat, continue a little further up Vicarage Lane to a footpath striking left. This doubles back up behind housing as a snicket to**

emerge into the fields. Cross to the far side of the large pasture, the path using a stile a little below the top corner. Joining a drive, go left on this to the secluded house at Ploverfield.

The enclosed way (Pennyunk Lane) rises past the house, and zigzags slavishly up between the fields to eventually empty into one of them. This is short-lived, for at the top the path turns right to become enclosed again at a dewpond, this time as a narrow footway. These gentle, wide landscapes lead to Longstone Edge across to the right. Intermittently enclosed now, it runs on to suddenly emerge above Monsal Dale, a supreme moment. Almost beneath our feet is the big sweeping bend of the Wye, with Upperdale running away upstream, and Cressbrook appearing beyond. Back downstream the river flows beneath Fin Cop, site of an Iron Age hillfort. The path run on the crest of the scrubby bank to Monsal Head, directly above the viaduct.

Monsal Head is popular with walkers and tourists alike, for it offers outstanding views down onto the Wye in Monsal Dale. The *Monsal Head Hotel* has a range of beers, gifts and crafts, and a cafe alongside. At the hotel cross the B6465 and head down the roadside footway into Little Longstone. En route we pass a chapel and the pinfold, where stray animals were held. At the bottom is the *Pack Horse*, a cosy little pub, and across the road, appropriately, a series of water troughs by the village pump. Just past here two paths strike off to the right. Take the first, which runs straight down the field then swings left to

run along to join the old railway line. Go left on it, and all that remains is to follow the Monsal Trail all the way back to Bakewell. Alternating between cuttings and small embankments, this is quite a nature trail.

The Monsal Trail was established by the National Park on the former Midland Railway's London to Manchester line. Trains ran from 1861 to 1968, after which the section from Matlock was axed. A decade of negotiations preceded the creation of an 8½ miles route from Blackwell Mill in Chee Dale to east of Bakewell. The trail was opened in 1981 and has seen many improvements to facilities along the way, with Miller's Dale station a focal point for visitors. Several sealed tunnels have footpath links that cleverly knit the trail together, so unlike other rail trails in the Peak, this one is not suitable for full use by cyclists. WALKS 9, 11, 12 and 17 take advantage of short sections of the trail. Long-term plans are afoot to re-open the line as a passenger service.

En route we pass Great Longstone station, with its two platforms and station house looking little changed. Beyond, the line bridges several roads and passes the architecturally intriguing Toll Bar House over to the left. At this point a bridleway crosses the line, and if followed right will lead directly down to Holme Bridge. Just past here the former Hassop station is reached, currently operating as a bookshop. It was built in 1863 a mile from the village, principally to serve Chatsworth House. Increasing signs of urbanisation lead back to Bakewell station.

Sheepwash Bridge,
Ashford in
the Water

HADDON HALL

START *Bakewell*   *Grid ref. SK 219686*

DISTANCE *5 miles*

ORDNANCE SURVEY MAPS
1:50,000
Landranger 119 - Buxton, Matlock & Dove Dale
1:25,000
Outdoor Leisure 24 - Peak District, White Peak

ACCESS *Start from the bridge in the town centre. Car parks alongside, downstream. Served by bus from most places, with regular services from Tideswell, Matlock, Buxton, Manchester and Sheffield.*

A gentle ramble around the environs of the lower Wye, with fine views and the major highlight of an outstanding historic house.

S   Bakewell is the true capital of the Peak, and largest settlement in the National Park. Its fine range of shops (including bookshops!) makes it ideal for a leisurely potter. A well to do air stems from the influence over many centuries of the Dukes of Rutland at nearby Haddon Hall. Unsuccessful attempts at creating a spa to rival Buxton were made in the late 17th century, and the Duke's bath house still exists. Focal point is Rutland Square where the *Rutland Arms*, a former coaching inn, stands: the old stables are across the road. The hotel is claimed as home of the celebrated Bakewell Pudding (incorrectly known as a 'Tart') which was created here in the mid-19th century when a cook misheard instructions about where to put her jam.

Outstanding in most views is the tall steeple of the parish church, with its unrivalled range of Anglo-Saxon, Norman and medieval grave stones and crosses: two Saxon crosses stand in the churchyard, one being a massive affair. The Vernon chapel has memorials to the

Manners family of Haddon. Another fine building is the early 17th century market hall, now a National Park visitor centre. Other historic buildings are Old House Museum (1543) and Bagshaw Hall (1684): both are within a stone's throw of the church, the Old Hall just above it, and the other just to the north, on Bagshaw Hill.

Perhaps the most attractive structure is the elegant bridge on the Wye, which complements the equally graceful river. Its five arches date back to the 14th century, and today sadly it suffers the indignity of a constant rumble of heavy traffic. Monday is market day, while in August Bakewell holds its famous one-day show, established in 1819.

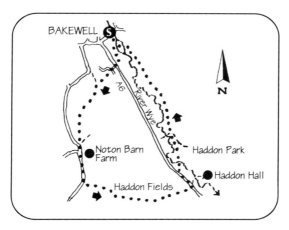

From the bridge head downstream on the town side of the Wye, past ducks awaiting their daily bread. Pass a footbridge over which the walk will conclude, and keep on to find a path into the park. Leave the river and cross the park to join the main road. Cross, and a little beyond a garage turn right along suburban Holywell. Jink right along Park Road, and as it bends right alongside Park View take a kissing-gate onto a snicket straight in front. This path climbs above the houses, through a few trees then along as a snicket past a cemetery to emerge onto a broad green way in front of school playing fields.

Go left through a couple of stiles then down the wall-side. In a variety of guises the path descends to cross a tiny stream. Down to the left note the impressive house, complete with clock tower, at Burton

Closes. **Beyond the stream the path bears right to a stile and gate, then slants up the field to find a stile in the hedge rising away. Now bear left to the far corner and continue as such up to the top corner.** By now we have superb views over the lower Wye, to Manners Wood and a first glimpse of Haddon Hall with Beeley Moor beyond, across the Derwent. **A bridle-gate admits onto a road: go left.**

Continue to enjoy the wide views, passing a junction and on to the brow beyond, where the road swings sharp right. An Ordnance Survey column along the wall to the left is the highest point of Haddon Fields. Go straight ahead on a track into a field. Turn first left and along the wallside to the corner. Haddon Hall is facing us across the valley. **Just past the corner is a stile, from where escape into a large, declining pasture.**

The hall is better seen ahead now, with Stanton Moor across to the right and Stanton in Peak village on its flank. Two grassy mounds in this field are suggestive of tumuli (burial sites), and the historic link is logical as the important White Peak road the Portway came this way, possibly in Bronze and Iron Age times. **Descend towards the bottom right corner, joining a wallside track beneath a stile. This runs down to a gate and resumes downhill past a walled, circular dewpond to the A6.** Throughout this section Haddon Hall looms ever larger and more impressive.

The entrance to the hall is directly across the road, through the arched gatehouse. It is open to the public (in season) and in many ways offers a more varied, interesting tour than Chatsworth, for all the larger house's undoubted splendour.

Haddon Hall is an outstanding, in national terms, medieval house. Dating back to the 12th century, it was added to by a long line of the Vernon family, who came over with William the Conqueror and spent 400 years here. In the mid-16th century it passed through marriage to the Manners family. As Earls of Rutland they progressed to a Dukedom in 1703, by which time Haddon was used only as second home to Belvoir Castle in Leicestershire. It was the ensuing period of two centuries largely untouched that have preserved the character of the old house. Finally sensitively restored by the 9th Duke in the early 20th century, it remains in the family to the present day. Most impressive are the courtyards overlooked by battlements, while the oldest part is the medieval chapel.

Cross and go left on the footway alongside the busy road, and at the first chance, an easily missed stile sends a footpath off into the trees. Between old fencing it runs down to an undistinguished footbridge on the Wye. Remain on this path which enjoys some riverside moments, wooded banks and islets before joining a surfaced drive alongside a bridge (Sheepbridge). Go right a few yards to a kissing-gate and resume upstream. The path runs above trees before being ushered onto the riverbank.

This pleasant section heads upstream, cutting ox-bows in the river and soon leaving it completely to remain with the right-hand hedgeside. A track forms and the way leads unfailingly on to enter the Bakewell showground. Beyond the show office a footbridge is reached over the millcut. Just ahead is the footbridge on the river, just short of the start point upstream.

Haddon Hall

LOG OF THE WALKS

WALK	DATE	NOTES
1		
2		
3		
4		
5		
6		
7		
8		
9		
10		
11		
12		
13		
14		
15		
16		
17		
18		
19		
20		

INDEX

Principal features: walk number refers

THE PEAK DISTRICT

Explore on foot Britain's most popular National Park with a comprehensive set of 5 guidebooks. Each contains 20 walks.

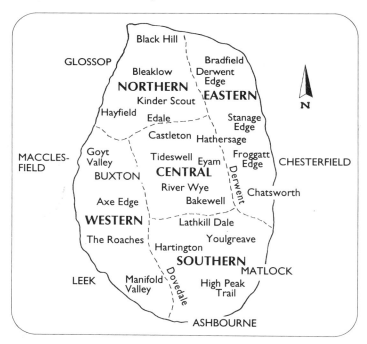

- **NORTHERN PEAK**   ISBN 1 870141 48 2
  Edale/Kinder Scout/Longdendale/Bleaklow/Hayfield/Mam Tor
- **EASTERN PEAK**   ISBN 1 870141 50 4
  Derwent Valley/Baslow/Eastern Edges/Chatsworth/Ladybower
- **CENTRAL PEAK**   ISBN 1 870141 51 2
  Bakewell/Wye Dale/Eyam/Monsal Dale/Tideswell/Miller's Dale
- **SOUTHERN PEAK**   ISBN 1 870141 52 0
  Dovedale/High Peak Trail/Lathkill Dale/Matlock/Tissington Trail
- **WESTERN PEAK**   ISBN 1 870141 54 7
  Buxton/The Roaches/Goyt Valley/Manifold Valley/Shutlingsloe

COOKS AND

CAMPAIGNERS

COMPENDIUM

THE WOMEN'S LIBRARY

celebrating and recording women's lives

Cooks and Campaigners Compendium

The Cooks and Campaigners Compendium is published
on the occasion of the Cooks and Campaigners exhibition
and the launch of **The Women's Library**

4 February – 13 July 2002

Published by
The Women's Library
Old Castle Street
London E1 7NT
t +44 (0)20 7320 2222
f +44 (0)20 7320 2333
www.thewomenslibrary.ac.uk

Exhibition and publication devised and organised by
Antonia Byatt
Chris Hammonds
Margot Heller
Deborah Smith
Louise Trodden

Designed by Herman Lelie, London
Typeset by Stefania Bonelli, London
Printed by PJ Print, London

Cover image: A suffrage garden party, *c.*1911

ISBN: 1-899764-24-0

Contents

INTRODUCTION

Introduction

The exhibition 'Cooks and Campaigners: An Introduction to The Women's Library' comes at a unique moment for the Library. It is the first time so much of our extraordinary collections has been displayed at the same time and it coincides with the opening of our new building in Old Castle Street. Built on the site of Whitechapel Wash Houses, the building has been designed by Wright & Wright to house the Library for the future. We hope the exhibition will reveal some of the history of the collections and lead people to explore them further in the beautiful research library upstairs.

By looking through our archives, examining the story of our library and how it has grown, it is possible to trace some of the major issues that have concerned women collectively over the last three hundred years or more. Many items on display were specifically designed to make a public impact, to be borne high in a march or worn proudly on a lapel. Other items are more intimate; recipes passed down from mother to daughter, personal diaries, the contents of a woman's purse removed from her body at the moment of her death. It is not possible to make definitive sense of women's lives over that period and looking at the display will raise as many questions as it gives answers. However, the library and its collections provide a remarkable window on to women's public and private lives.

The Library grew out of the London Society for Women's Suffrage, which was founded in 1867. It started its formal life as a Library with the appointment of Vera Douie, its first Librarian, in 1926, and headquarters in Marsham Street, with a café and lecture theatre. Subsequently, the Library was renamed The Fawcett Library after Millicent Garrett Fawcett. She had been the president of the National Union of Women's Suffrage Societies and campaigned for the vote constitutionally, persisting throughout World War I, and beyond. Much of our suffrage material derives from these connections.

After the vote was won, the Library became a useful resource for women who were hoping to enter the professions. It provided them with information and fodder to further their careers, and was often used by policy makers to gather statistics about women's employment and pay. Vera Douie, who worked for the Library for 41 years, relied on donations to build up the Library and she wrote letters to many prominent women asking them to contribute. Both Virginia Woolf and Vera Brittain were among these supporters, often visiting the Library and working there. As the Library developed other collections were donated, including the Cavendish Bentinck Library in 1931 which contains much of our 17th and 18th century material, the Sadd Brown Library in 1939 named after the suffragette Myra Sadd Brown, and the Josephine Butler Society Library in 1951.

Some people still remember the Library in its first home in Marsham Street, and its second in an old pub in Wilton Street, where the Librarian's desk strongly resembled a bar. In 1977, after a steep rise in rent, the Library moved to what was then City of London Polytechnic, saved by the joint efforts of Cynthia White and Rita Pankhurst, and supported by the Friends of the Fawcett Library, who subsequently raised much of the funding that supplemented its existence at the Polytechnic (which became London Guildhall University).

A suffrage fund-raising garden party, *c*.1911

The Library was, however, always short of funds, and relied on the commitment of the women who used it and saw it as essential. We are not the only library about women in the country, but we are the largest. Much has changed in women's lives since the Library was founded, and for that reason many see its role as crucial, documenting a major part of recent social history. There wasn't money to build the collection grandly, but many people have contributed books, archives and objects to it over the years. This can give the collections a maverick feel, but that is part of their joy. The Library has certainly inspired commitment in its staff as well as its users and Friends. The last Librarian, David Doughan, served the Library for 23 years, building its collections and commanding an extraordinary knowledge of women's campaigning.

Since 1977 the Library has lived in a basement at London Guildhall University, hard to find, charming but cramped. Visitors from all over the world have visited it, but so has rain and, even worse, sewage. After the third flood the University decided the Library must be rehoused in order to survive and successfully applied for a grant from The Heritage Lottery Fund. In 1998 £4.2m was awarded and building started on the site of the old Wash Houses in Old Castle Street. The new five-story building is the realisation of a dream for the people who have built and cared for the Library over the last 75 years.

'Cooks and Campaigners' offers a glimpse of what can be found in the new Library. Though our strength lies in the suffrage collections we felt it was important to illustrate the breadth of subjects addressed. We've organised the collections into approachable categories – Work, Law, Health, Fashion and Lifestyle, Cookery, Travel and Suffrage. They overlap and lead into each other, offering different routes into the concerns of the Library, demonstrating how much has changed in women's lives and how much has remained the same.

We've also tried to choose some of the most visually arresting material, since many of our objects, posters and textiles were designed to catch people's attention. Whether beautiful, disturbing or witty they tell an unforgettable story of causes that either seem unbelievable now (women disenfranchised) or which linger on (domestic violence), but they are also an interesting record of the techniques used to bring those points home. Many of our banners were designed to be the right weight for women to carry, to be objects of beauty which could be exhibited as well as paraded. Together with many of the posters, magazines and other campaigning paraphernalia, they belie a view held by some that the women's movement has been over earnest. Often produced by small collectives and campaigning groups, it is easy to imagine the hours, comradery and passion put into such enterprises.

The Library will continue to grow. It is quite clear from looking at 'Cooks and Campaigners' that there are gaps in our collections. They do not reflect the experiences of all women in Britain by any means and in the future we will strive to do that better. We may guess at the campaigns of tomorrow, from genetic engineering to the work/life balance, but some will be hidden from our view. The new building is a place for people to debate and explore what the future may hold for women. The Library has been built through the active support of many women and men over the years; now that we have space to grow we hope people will continue to help us build our collections. The story of our collections is not over.

Antonia Byatt, Director

CAMPAIGNING

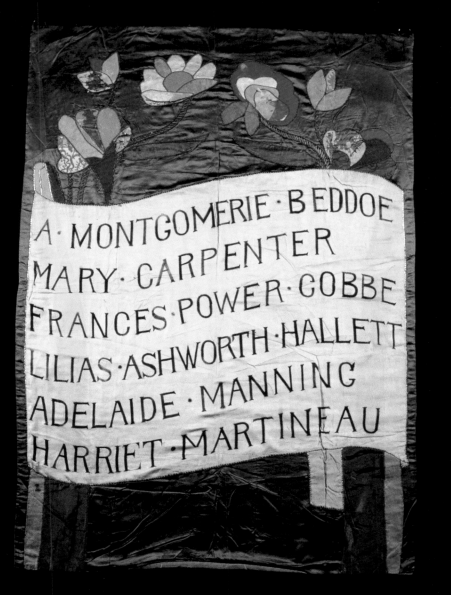

A · MONTGOMERIE · BEDDOE
MARY · CARPENTER
FRANCES · POWER · COBBE
LILIAS · ASHWORTH · HALLETT
ADELAIDE · MANNING
HARRIET · MARTINEAU

The irony looks embarrassingly heavy-handed now. But back in 1971, when I returned from school in the Caribbean to a male dominated university, I learnt that in post-*Female Eunuch* London men were men and women were for recreation. Even in Imperial College, the elite science campus – geek city, really – people actually lived this rubbish. Manliness was measured in yards of ale; social standing secured by pinning women's knickers behind the men-only (yes men-only) Student Union bar. And we were probably the brightest of our generation – the place was stiff with past and future Nobel prize winners. We changed it, of course, and today's students would be appalled. But one sobering thought – we who tolerated this for so long are now in charge. Have we really changed?

Trevor Phillips

11, Downing Street,
Whitehall.S.W.

30th November, 1911.

My dear Mrs. Fawcett,

(I thank you for your appreciative note, which I value
very much coming from you.) I have been very unhappy
about the prospects during the last few days. The action
of the Militants is alienating sympathy from the women's
cause in every quarter: I felt the depressing influence
even at the meeting at Bath. Tuesday's violence and last
night's indecent exhibition, when the Prime Minister
supporting a charitable institution was howled down in a
place of worship, have between them created a very grave
situation. If next year's chances of carrying either a
women's amendment or a Bill are not to be totally ruined
some emphatic action must be taken at once. You can
hardly realise what the feeling is even amongst Members
of Parliament who have hitherto been steadiest in their
support of Women's Suffrage. I feel confident that if
these tactics are persisted in our hopes of being able
to secure the ~~(confirmation)~~ insertion of a Women's
Suffrage amendment in next year's Bill will be of the
slightest. I have consulted Sir Edward Grey and other
friends of the movement and they take an equally serious
view of the situation. What do you suggest? Anti-
Suffragists are of course exultant. ~~(and I)~~ They feel
confident that the effect of our agitation will be
neutralised by the antics of the Militants.

Very sincerely yours,

(signed) D. Lloyd George
Mrs. Henry Fawcett.

Women's Social and Political Union 'branded' tea set, *c.*1910
Its delicate design of prison chains and winged angel evokes a poignant
Edwardian elegance. The tea set is just visible in the photograph of the very
respectable bring-and-buy fundraising garden-party (cover image), replete
with well-ironed tablecloths, boaters and serious millinery.

Jill Liddington

Justice at the door, poster designed by Mary Lowndes, 1912

If Mary Lowndes came back today, would Britannia still be outside the door? With only 18% of MPs being women, surely the door is still only ajar and Justice merely on the threshold?

Helen Carey

WIGAN ELECTION.

A PUBLIC

MEETING

WILL BE HELD ON

THURSDAY, JAN. 6th, 1881,

IN THE

PUBLIC HALL, KING STREET,

TO PROMOTE THE UNCONDITIONAL REPEAL

OF THE

CONTAGIOUS DISEASES ACTS

RELATING TO WOMEN.

CHAIR TO BE TAKEN AT 8 O'CLOCK.

THE MEETING WILL BE ADDRESSED BY

J. BIRBECK NEVINS, Esq, M.D.

OF LIVERPOOL;

T. CARSON, Esq., M.R.C.S.I.

OF LIVERPOOL;

WILLIAM T. SWAN, Esq.

OF LONDON, REPRESENTATIVE OF THE NORTHERN COUNTIES LEAGUE FOR THE ABOLITION OF STATE REGULATION OF VICE.

EDMUND JONES,

PRESIDENT OF THE NATIONAL WORKMEN'S LEAGUE FOR REPEAL OF THE CONTAGIOUS DISEASES ACTS.

ELECTORS! No question upon which either Mr. LANCASTER or Mr. POWELL will have to record his Vote, if returned to Parliament, is of greater importance than whether the one-sided, unjust, and unconstitutional CONTAGIOUS DISEASES ACTS, 1866-9, should continue to disgrace our Statute Book, or be unconditionally repealed.

Every Voter, Liberal or Conservative, is earnestly invited.

WALL, PRINTER, WALLGATE, WIGAN.

At 1:30 am on April 21, 1881, Josephine Butler was in the Ladies' Gallery when, after an all-night debate, the acts were at last repealed by a majority vote of 182 to 110.

Margaret Forster

Coming In With The Tide, designed by Emily J. Harding Andrews, Published by the Artists' Suffrage League, c.1908

COMING IN WITH THE TIDE

During the Great Storm of 1824, Mrs Partington, a latter-day Cnut, was reputed to have sought to keep the Atlantic Ocean at bay with her broom. This symbol of reaction had been used during the campaign for political reform in the early 1830s, demonstrating the inevitability of change.

Angela V. John

Campaign poster issued by the Contraception Action Programme from the Equal Opportunities Commission collection, c.1979

SO LONG AS WOMEN ARE NOT FREE THE PEOPLE ARE NOT FREE

Campaign poster from the Equal Opportunities Commission collection, c.1980

The women's liberation movement made a new kind of politics out of daily life. It translated the oppressive details of existence into a protest which combined working conditions with personal relationships, challenged state policy and talked about loving.

Sheila Rowbotham

Women's Suffrage poster, published by the Suffrage Atelier, c.1912

It's an image of power and potential in waiting – to be achieved within the decade.

Kate Adie

The Government responded [to hunger strikes] by forcibly feeding the women, a procedure justified as necessary 'hospital treatment' to save lives but which the hunger strikers experienced as torture.

June Purvis

Equal Rights, 1 October 1932

Equal Rights

VOL. XVIII, No. 35
FIVE CENTS

SATURDAY
OCTOBER 1, 1932

Courtesy International News.

Amelia Earhart at the White House

This picture was taken after the Equal Rights Conference which Miss Earhart had with the President. She was accompanied by Mrs. Harvey W. Wiley, National Chairman, National Woman's Party, and Anita Pollitzer, Vice-Chairman.

Equal Pay demonstration outside the Houses of Parliament, 1954

Greenham Common campaign poster, 1981–91

Poster for Spare Rib, 1972

LAW

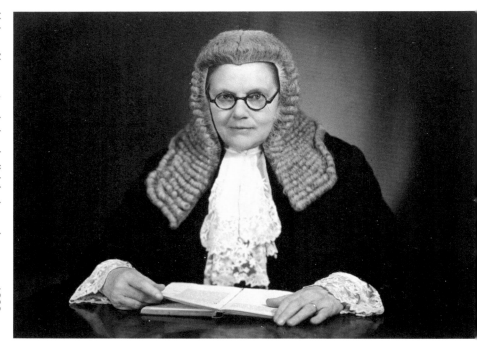

Helena Normanton in her judicial wig and gown, c.1922

I felt an immediate bond with Helena Normanton when I heard about her battle to keep her maiden name both professionally and as a private citizen… As she pointed out in one of her articles the use of one's maiden name is an old English practice – everyone has heard of Anne Boleyn, Catherine Howard and Catherine Parr… As she summed up: 'Whatever King Henry VIII may have done in the way of removing his Queen's heads, it never occurred to him to remove and obliterate the name they were born to'.

Cherie Booth QC

Crown Office Row.
Middle Temple.
London. E.C.
Nov 21 1924

Dear Normanton

Not only myself but some
other members of the Bar who
have consistently remained
opposed to its entry by women
desire to point out that the
culmination we most feared viz
an increase of the jealousy which
has always been a feature of legal life
— has occurred and that most
prominently in connection with yourself It is
felt that the time has arrived when
you should seriously consider what you

Common Room.
Middle Temple.
London.E.C.

Nov 21 1924

Dear Normanton

Not only myself but some other members of the Bar who
have consistently remained opposed to its entry by
women desire to point out that the culmination we most
feared viz an increase of the jealousy which has always
been a feature of legal life — has occurred and that
most prominently in connection with yourself. It is felt
that the time has arrived when you should seriously
consider what some will do to limit and lessen the
amount of gossip in circulation about yourself.

No doubt your partial successes have caused the other
women envy so this letter is not sent in any spirit of
censure. but are you _really_ so unaware as you seem to
be of the origin of the comments upon you? There was
trouble at Winchester and also at Clerkenwell. In every
case those starting it have had one feature in common
they have been friends of Miss Ashford; nor is it any
secret that she openly makes statements about your mode
of life, literary work, marriage, and what is most
important to us, your professional code which unless
true have gone in the opinion of many, more than far
enough. They are not we think to any extent true but
your own impassity is being remarked upon.

We are informed that there has been a letter sent to
the Bar Council about some action of yours and this lady
has the credit — if there be any credit in one barrister
reporting another to the Bar Council (it is such an
unpleasing novelty induced by feminine jealousy) — of being
the true inspirer of it. Although the letter is said to
have fallen very flat and merely to have bored the Council
yet the malevolence of the intention is very plain.

Those taking the liberty of advising you in this letter
do at least recommend that you do not continue to ask
this lady to your house and to treat her as if she was a
valued friend. Such friendliness is much misunderstood in
a world where people are expected to guard their honour
closely, especially and above all in our profession.

We hope you will not resent this letter. We are acquainted
with the results of the searching and satisfactory enquiry
held by the late Sir Robert Muir into your professional
behaviour. But you are not being prudent in ignoring what
is going on now. The lady mentioned should either withdraw
or substantiate.

We ask you to consider this letter primarily from the
point of view of our great profession and secondarily
from your own. This letter is unsigned simply because
it represents the views of a group of barristers not of
one but we can all say we are (reserving the question
of the desirability of women in the profession)

Yours Wellwishers

THE LAW & THE MOTHER.

MARRIED MOTHER: "The magistrate says I am not the parent of my own child! so my old man has to lose a day's work to get the Vaccination Exemption Order for the baby"

UNMARRIED MOTHER: "That's queer, I'm counted the parent of my baby all right; the Law don't seem to treat you very well."

Published by the Suffrage ATELIER, 1, Pembroke Cottages, Edwardes Square, Kensington, London, W.

HOW THE LAW 'PROTECTS THE DAUGHTERS.'

ENGLISH GIRLS (Crying): "Nurse says we had better get used to the baby brother taking our things, because when we grow up we sha'nt have anything, he will take it all."

FRENCH GIRLS: "What a shame; the brothers and sisters have equal shares in our Country."

Published by the Suffrage ATELIER, 1, Pembroke Cottages, Edwardes Square, Kensington, London, W.

How The Law Protects the Daughters, published by the Suffrage Atelier, c.1909

WORK

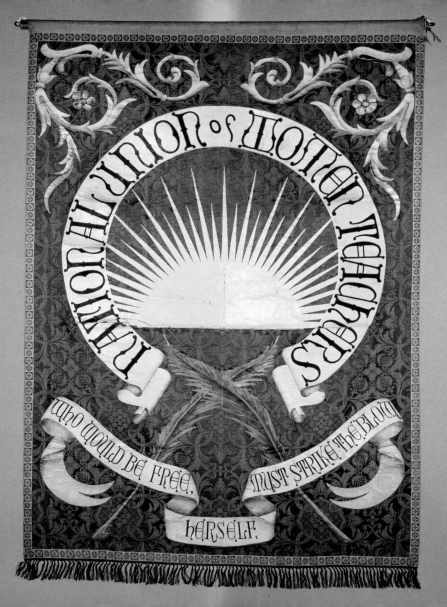

NATIONAL UNION of WOMEN TEACHERS

WHO WOULD BE FREE, MUST STRIKE THE BLOW

HERSELF.

This campaign for equality at work goes back into the 19th century and stretches into the 21st. Women now have equality with men in career after career. They even have equal status in some religious organisations. But the Church of England resisted – even whilst its sister church, the Church of Ireland, had no problem with women clergy. The Movement for the Ordination of Women has had some success, but there is still much to do. Women Bishops in Britain, female Rabbis for Orthodox Jews, female Imams in Islam – it's all to play for.

Julia Neuberger

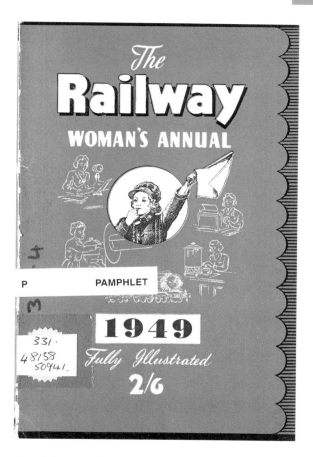

An aviation student went up for her license, and found the inspector very tough. Instead of being content with the usual landings he made her come into a spot. Again and again she hit the spot accurately, but, instead of passing her, he kept on sending her up, moving the spot each time. And each time she'd slide right into it. Finally the inspector gave up. 'Okay, she'll do,' he said. 'But I tell you it's a miracle.'

From 'Aviation – A Career for Girls', Amy Johnson, in *What Shall I Be?*, Collins, 1938

Ford Machinists strike over Equal Pay, 1968

Women Underpaid – Men Out of Work, published by the Suffrage Atelier, c.1914

WOMEN UNDERPAID - - MEN OUT OF WORK.

Jones "Our Guvnor don't want women to get the vote because their wages would go up; I'm often out of work but my missis and the girls can always get a job but the pay don't keep one let alone a family! LET'S HELP TO GET THEM THE VOTE AND A LIVING WAGE."

Mrs Doreen Hamilton has seven children… and a full-time job in teaching, on top of which she goes to evening classes and does church work. Everyone in her family does a part of the housework: duties are written up on a notice-board… On Saturday the week's menus are planned… Each night, dirty clothes are sorted to put in the automatic washing machine and tumble-dried the next morning. Those needing mending are done next evening. Daily, two beds have their linen changed. Weekly, a pair of net curtains is washed. One room a week is spring-cleaned between Christmas and summer… The children have to tidy their rooms and, in turn, lay table and wash-up in a dishwasher … Mr Hamilton (also a teacher) cleans all shoes, lays breakfast, stokes the boiler. The result of this clockwork routine is that adequate leisure time is assured for everybody, and no one person bears the whole burden.

From 'Keeping Housework Down' in *Jobs For Mothers*, Elizabeth Gundrey, 1967, Hodder and Stoughton

Strike While the Iron is Hot! from the Equal Opportunities Commission collection, c.1982

FASHION
AND LIFESTYLE

JOAN OF ARC

SANS PEUR ET
SANS REPROCHE

Advertisement for Holmes shoes in *Vogue*, 16 October 1965

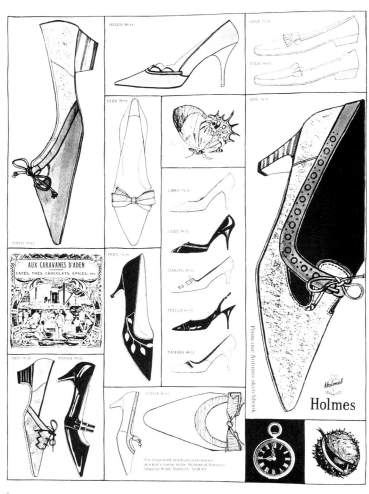

Housewife

Sixpence   VOL 2 N⁰ 6 JUNE

Portrait of Mary Quant by John Adriaan, early 1960's

The days Women
rocked the World
Georgie Best on Sex
Does the Government
care about Pensioners?
Richard Neville
on the Glossies
Growing up in the
Bosom Boom
8 page News Section
and lots more inside.

First issue of *Spare Rib*, July 1972

When we started *Spare Rib* we had no idea what an
institution it would become and that the name would
live on forever… At the beginning, we really thought
feminism meant liberation for both sexes and that the
lot of being a bloke was pretty ghastly too.

Rosie Boycott

SOMETHING TO SHOUT ABOUT!

No. 582 MARCH 1st 1975 · THURSDAY · 5p

Jackie

FOR THOUGHTS OF LOVE

No. 590 APRIL 26th 1975 · THURSDAY · 5p

Jackie

LOOK AT THE LOVE
Super romantic fashions
he can't resist!
SKIN-FEEL LOVE TO TOUCH
How to be a smoothie!
Find out inside
MEET JENNY FROM JACKIE
She does things
you'd love to!

When I was seventeen and looking for a job I saw an advert in the *Evening Standard* for teenage writers. I was a teenager and I very much wanted to be a writer so I sent them a jokey article. To my astonishment and delight the magazine company, DC Thomsons of Dundee, paid me the very Victorian fee of three guineas and offered me a job on their new teenage magazine.

I was a shy girl from the London suburbs but the company thought I was part of the swinging sixties scene. They decided they'd give their new magazine my name – *Jackie*.

Jacqueline Wilson

48

'Brotherly Love', photo-lovestory from *Jackie*, 22 October 1988

Brotherly Love continued on Page 13

JACKIE 9

49

COOKERY

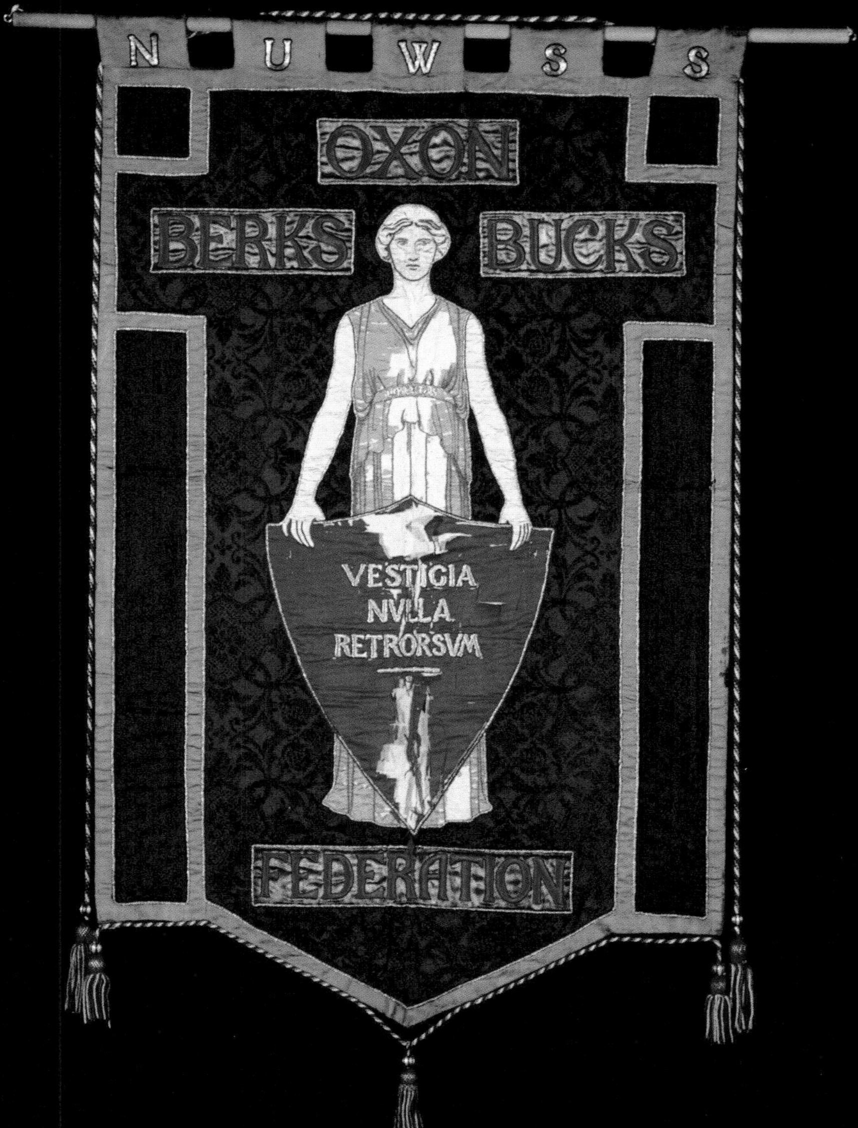

Banner of the Oxfordshire, Buckinghamshire and Berkshire Federation of the NUWSS, designed by the Artists' Suffrage League, 1908

NUWSS

OXON

BERKS · BUCKS

VESTIGIA
NVLLA
RETRORSVM

FEDERATION

Recipes for Lovers, Barbara Cartland, Corgi, 1977

If I had married Barbara Cartland style; in white lace, in a church, after a long engagement, would my marriage have lasted more than twenty-five years? My boyfriend David suggested we get married on Tuesday at four in the morning, we did so on the Friday at Kensington Registry Office, where I wore a pink mini coat from Biba…

I may not have married in the way Barbara Cartland would have advised, I may not have given my husband a buttonhole on each anniversary or cooked him a classic three course dinner – and we may not have got beyond our Silver Wedding. But I have many good times to remember, three lovely children, and an ex-husband who is still my close friend. So maybe I have a chance of living happily ever after.

Josceline Dimbleby

SPECIAL OCCASIONS

A PINK DINNER is a lovely way of celebrating the first time you met or the first time you made love. Have pink candles on the table and pink flowers, pink table-napkins, and of course wear a pink dress.

MENU

TROUT IN PINK COAT

PINK CHICKEN

STRAWBERRY ICE CREAM
HOT RASPBERRY SAUCE

COFFEE

WINE: Lanson Pink Champagne
or
Vin Rosé

LIQUEUR: Rosé

113

'A Pink Dinner', Barbara Cartland with Nigel Gordon taken from *Recipes for Lovers*, Barbara Cartland. Reproduced by arrangement with Rupert Crew Ltd.

'An Apple a Day' in *She* magazine, May 1963

AN APPLE A DAY . . .

*Two lovely ways of keeping
the doctor at bay*

Salmon Mousse

Cost: about 9/6 Serves 4

1 oz. butter; 1 tbs. finely chopped onion; 1 oz. flour; ½ pt. milk; thyme, bayleaf, nutmeg; ½ lb. salmon (tinned or fresh); 1 level dsp. gelatine; 2 oz. stoned chopped black olives; 2 sticks celery, diced; 2 tbs. tomato ketchup; 3 tbs. mayonnaise; salt and pepper to taste; 1 lb. red eating apples; juice of 1 lemon; ½ cucumber, black olives, watercress (for decoration).

Melt butter in saucepan and gently fry the chopped onion until transparent, but not brown. Stir in flour and cook gently for 3 mins. Add milk gradually, stirring all the time. Add thyme (in a piece of muslin), bayleaf, grated nutmeg. Simmer over a low heat for 10 mins. Remove herbs and cool sauce.

Flake salmon finely and gradually beat into the sauce. Add gelatine, dissolved in 2 tbs. water, chopped olives, celery and ¼ diced red eating apple. Stir in tomato ketchup and mayonnaise and season to taste with salt and pepper. Pile into a serving dish and chill.

Just before serving, decorate with rest of apples cut into slices and dipped in lemon juice to retain colour. Fill the centre of the dish with black olives, finely sliced cucumber and watercress.

Open Apple-Cream Pie

Cost: about 6/6 Serves 4-6

For the pastry:	For the filling:
8 oz. plain flour	6 tart apples
Pinch salt	6 oz. sugar
2 oz. margarine	1 oz. flour
2 oz. lard	½ tsp. salt
Water to bind	½ tsp. cinnamon
	½ pt. double cream

Make pastry by sieving the flour and salt together. Rub in the fats until the mixture resembles fine breadcrumbs. Add enough water to bind and knead lightly. Roll to fit a 9-inch pie dish. Prick well and bake blind for 10 mins. at 425°F. Mk 6. Slice the apples thinly. Mix the 6 oz. sugar, flour, salt and cinnamon, add to the apples and toss together lightly. Place in the pastry shell and bake for a further 20 mins. Pour the cream over pie, and bake for another 10 mins. Serve with extra cream.

'Fish fingers? I didn't know fishes had fingers'"

Preserves

LEMON CURD.

Recipe. 2 ozs. butter.
Rind and juice of two lemons.
3 ozs. sugar.
2 eggs.

Method.
Melt butter in saucepan, wash lemons, grate rind then squeeze juice. Add to butter in pan along with sugar.
Beat the eggs and add, stirring well with a wooden spoon. Heat very slowly. Remove from heat as soon as the mixture thickens.
Pour into jars, cover and label.

MINCEMEAT.

Recipe.

4 ozs. raisins.	Rind and juice of 1 lemon.
4 ozs. sultanas.	½ teasp. ground nutmeg.
4 ozs. currants.	½ teasp. cinnamon.
4 ozs. suet.	½ teasp. ground ginger.
4 ozs. brown sugar.	½ teasp. mixed spice.
2 ozs. mixed peel.	¼ teasp. salt.
2 apples.	

Method.
Wash and pick over raisins, currants and sultanas, removing stalks.
Split, stone and chop raisins. Prepare apples (page 50) and chop finely. Add chopped suet and chopped peel. Grate lemon rind and squeeze juice. Put all ingredients into mixing bowl. Measure spices, sugar and salt. Mix all together thoroughly then press into jars, cover and label.

86

HEALTH

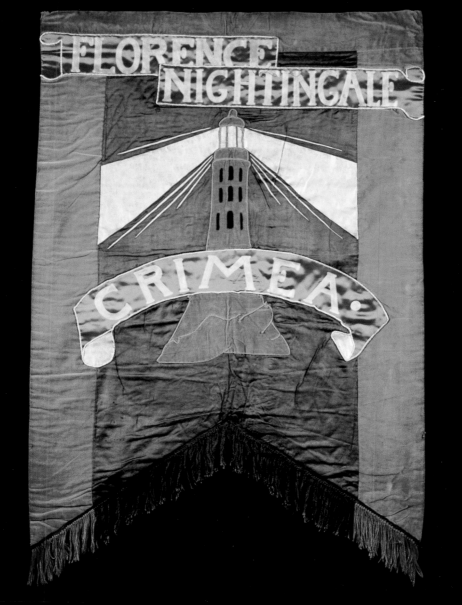

FLORENCE NIGHTINGALE

CRIMEA.

Our Bodies, Ourselves, The Boston Women's Health Book Collective, 1971

'A man who does not know sick women,' one Victorian doctor wrote, 'does not know women'. Medical history is certainly part of women's history, and we could certainly argue that someone who does not know the history of sick women does not understand much about women generally. As the Boston Women's Collective phrased it in their pioneering medical self-help books for women, *Our Bodies, Ourselves*. But what is 'illness'? Does it include menstruation, pregnancy, childbirth, and menopause? What about exercise and fitness? How have these natural aspects of the female life cycle been treated by medicine, and by feminism in the past?… As women – ourselves – have played a greater role in medicine and health, we have certainly learned more about women's bodies and minds, and challenged much of the conventional wisdom of male medicine.

Elaine Showalter

OUR BODIES, OURSELVES

WOMEN UNITE

A BOOK
BY AND
FOR
WOMEN

REVISED AND EXPANDED

OVERSIZE ~STON WOMEN'S HEALTH BOOK COLLECTIVE $4.95

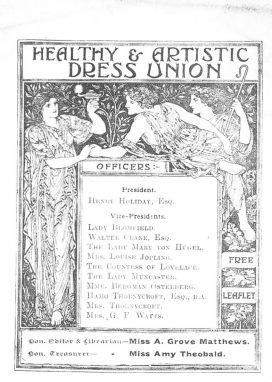

HEALTHY & ARTISTIC DRESS UNION

OFFICERS :—

President.
HENRY HOLIDAY, ESQ.

Vice-Presidents.
LADY BLOMFIELD.
WALTER CRANE, ESQ.
THE LADY MARY VON HÜGEL.
MRS. LOUISE JOPLING.
THE COUNTESS OF LOVELACE.
THE LADY MUNCASTER.
MME. BERGMAN OSTERBERG.
HAMO THORNYCROFT, ESQ., R.A.
MRS. THORNYCROFT.
MRS. G. F. WATTS.

FREE

LEAFLET

Hon. Editor & Librarian—**Miss A. Grove Matthews.**
Hon. Treasurer—   -   **Miss Amy Theobald.**

How to Dress Without the Corset.

THOSE who are asked to give up wearing the corset generally complain that it is impossible to dress comfortably without it; that its disuse means catching cold, great untidiness in appearance and in fact, general discomfort. All these points I hope to meet in this paper, giving what practical suggestions I can from my own experience, as one who for three years wore corsets and at the end of that time abolished them, and in consequence was obliged to reform her clothing.

TOO GREAT A RISK!

Too Great a Risk!, The Family Planning Association

Too Great a Risk!, The Family Planning Association

TRAVEL

DARE TO BE FREE

WOMENS LEAGUE FREEDOM

I've spent most of my adult life travelling for pleasure, often combining a trip with walking. I've walked in the Himalayas, Australia, New Zealand, France, Spain, America, the Caribbean, and of course, all over the British Isles. I've always kept diaries and scrapbooks of my travels, just like the formidable group of Victorian lady travellers who toured everywhere from India to Russia. This kind of travel is a middle class luxury, compared to the poor women who joined the British Women's Emigration Association. They crossed the world in search of decent jobs and the possibility of meeting a husband – both of which were in short supply in Britain. They travelled out of economic necessity, leaving family and friends behind. The hazards facing the lone female travelling in Britain led to the setting up of the Traveller's Aid Society. We've got them to thank for Ladies waiting rooms on stations, now sadly few and far between. Is travelling alone at night in contemporary Britain any safer than it was in Victorian times? A lot of women might not agree.

Women in Britain did not have the vote, but it didn't stop the rich and upper middle class adventuresses from packing their trunks and taking off to the tropics. Maude Royden met everyone from Ghandi downwards. Harriet White-Fisher and Lady Annie Brassey were two more intrepid females in search of thrills abroad. Back In Britain the idea of travel guides to beautiful areas like the Lake District was taking off, and women leapt at the chance to explore. Travel then, as now, was a way of escaping the dreary routine of day to day life, and a chance to broaden your mind and meet a wider circle of people. For Victorian women travel was a liberating experience, just as it is to me.

Janet Street-Porter

glass — windows but plastic bags
the fields are weeded perfectly —
lots of orchards with apple trees &
very well-kept vegetable gardens
yet no sanitation & dirt everywhere
— downs. Outside immaculately
stacked & stacked firewood — the
mols of art hard to understand.
30 short but arrow as long downward
eh. fact of I plan to pee on plant
my a balcony if desperate at night
When I asked Ang how as a Buddhist he
could eat meat he ate the chicken he said he just
did extra chanting the next day & asked
for forgiveness 3 times — hypocrite!

Monday 13th April
Today is Nepali new year apparently
tho we see little sign of holiday —
lots of people (mostly women) hard at
work as usual.
The fluorescent lights went out at 10pm
last night when the generator stopped
but we were fast asleep

The
Imperial Colonist

THE OFFICIAL ORGAN OF
THE BRITISH WOMEN'S EMIGRATION ASSOCIATION AND
THE SOUTH AFRICAN COLONISATION SOCIETY.

THE SETTLER'S WIFE.

Among the Australian poets an honourable place was earned some years ago by Victor Daley. The following verse from his pen goes far towards epitomising the lives of many settlers' wives "out back," who play a brave part in bearing the White Woman's Burden.

She helped him make a little home,
Where miles were gum trees gaunt and stark
And blue-bush, and waved green feathered form,
Working from dawn of day till dark
Till that dark forest formed a frame
For vineyards that the Gods might bless,
And what was savage once became
An Eden in the Wilderness.

| VOL. IX | APRIL, 1911. | No. 112. |

Notes of the Month.

Their Royal Highnesses the Duke and Duchess of Connaught have been graciously pleased to give their patronage to the British Women's Emigration Association.

British Women's Emigration Association Annual Meeting.

A crowded and successful meeting was held by kind permission of Lord and Lady Salisbury, at 20, Arlington Street, on Monday, March 20th. Sir Reginald Talbot (late Governor of Victoria) presided, and in the course of a thoughtful speech, emphasised very strongly the need for protection for our girls on the long voyage to Australasia. Dr. Parkin spoke with his accustomed eloquence, and with an earnestness which could not fail to impress his hearers. Mrs. Bevan made a very amusing speech on the great need for women in Canada as observed by her in a recent journey across the Dominion—and Canon Beal described life on the prairie and spoke some very wise words as to the hardships women have to face. A short speech by Mrs. Brodrick on the financial situation of the Association, and a vote of thanks to Lord and Lady Salisbury and the speakers

Pages from *The Imperial Colonist* Vol.10, No.12, Lady Knightley of Fawsley (ed.), The British Women's Emigration Association, 1911

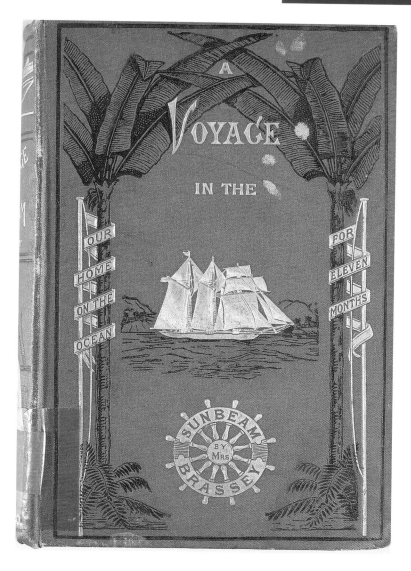

A Voyage in the 'Sunbeam', Mrs. Brassey, Longmans, Green & Co., 1881

'Cooks and Campaigners' Selectors

Grateful thanks to all the exhibition Selectors.

Kate Adie first came to the nation's attention for her frontline journalism and news broadcasts. She is the chief news correspondent for the BBC.

Isabella Blow is the former Fashion Editor of *The Sunday Times* and contributing Fashion Editor of *The Face*.

Yasmin Alibhai-Brown is a Senior Research Fellow at the Foreign Policy Centre, a writer and a broadcaster. Her books include *Mixed Feelings* and *Who Do We Think We Are?*

Melissa Benn is a journalist and writer commenting on women's lives. Her books include *Madonna and Child* and *The Rape Controversy*.

Iwona Blazwick is Director of The Whitechapel Art Gallery.

Cherie Booth QC is a prominent barrister.

Rosie Boycott is a journalist and writer. She was founder Editor of the women's liberation magazine *Spare Rib* and was Editor of *The Express*.

Helen Carey is the National Chair of the National Federation of Women's Institutes.

Barbara Castle served in several Labour Governments, spearheading many reforms including those on equal pay. Her books include *Sylvia and Christabel Pankhurst*.

Bronwyn Cosgrave is a writer, journalist and Features Editor for British *Vogue*.

Edwina Currie was Minister for Health under Margaret Thatcher and has written many best selling novels including *Chasing Men*.

Jeremy Deller is an artist who works with groups as diverse as break-dancers, pensioners and miners. His reconstruction of 'The Battle of Orgreave' was made last year for Channel 4.

Josceline Dimbleby is a food writer and TV chef and has written a number of cookery books.

David Doughan was Reference Librarian of the Fawcett Library until April 2000.

Margaret Forster is a novelist, biographer and literary critic. Her recent best selling works include a biography of *Daphne du Maurier*, a memoir *Hidden Lives* and the novel *The Memory Box*.

Roderick Floud is Provost of London Guildhall University.

Susan Greenfield is Director of The Royal Institution of Great Britain.

Bonnie Greer is a playwright, fiction writer and cultural critic regularly appearing on *Late Review*. Her books include *Eating Guts with Princess Di*.

Loyd Grossman is known for hosting programmes such as *Through the Keyhole* and *Masterchef*.

Angela V. John lectures at Greenwich University and is co-editor of *The Men's Share? Masculinities, male support and female suffrage, 1890–1920*.

Helena Kennedy QC is a leading barrister and Chair of the British Council.

Martha Kearney presents Woman's Hour and is political editor of BBC2's *Newsnight*.

Sarah Kent is an art critic and Arts Editor for *Time Out*.

Jill Liddington is Reader in Gender History at Leeds University and is co-author of *One Hand Tied Behind Us*.

Bill Morris is the General Secretary of the Transport and General Workers Union.

Jenni Murray presents Woman's Hour on Radio 4. Her books include *A History of Women Since World War II*.

Rabbi Julia Neuberger was Britain's first woman Rabbi and is Chief Executive of the King's Fund.

Maureen Paley is Director of Interim Art, London.

Marguerite Patten has been a cookery writer, demonstrator and home economist and first appeared on television in 1947. She has written over 165 cookery books.

Susan Philipsz is an artist based in Belfast and has produced a new commission as part of 'Cooks and Campaigners'.

Trevor Phillips has worked in television and is Deputy Chair of the London Assembly, a Labour Party Councillor and former President of the National Union of Students.

Kate Pullinger is presently Writing Fellow at The Women's Library and author of *The Last Time I Saw Jane*, *Where Does Kissing End?* and *Weird Sister*.

June Purvis is Professor of Women's and Gender History at the University of Portsmouth. She has edited *Votes for Women* with Sandra Holton.

Mary Quant is a fashion designer who became synonymous with the fashions of the swinging sixties most famously launching the mini skirt.

Claire Rayner has worked as an Agony Aunt in publications such as *Women's Own* and *Woman* and appeared on radio and television.

Rose Gray & Ruth Rogers operate The River Café, one of the best known restaurants in London, and have published two editions of The River Café Cook Book.

Michele Roberts is a Booker Prize nominated author and poet. Her most recent novel, *Fair Exchange*, looks at the experience of women during the French Revolution.

Sheila Rowbotham is an academic and writer and was a leading figure in the women's movement in the 1970s and 1980s. Her books include *A Century of Women: The History of Women in Britain and the US*.

Will Self has written a number of best-selling novels including *Great Apes*, *The Quantity Theory of Insanity* and *How the Dead Live*.

Elaine Showalter is Professor of English at Princeton University. Her books include *A Literature of Their Own: British Women Novelists from Bronte to Lessing*.

Janet Street-Porter is 'Editor at large' for the *Independent on Sunday* and is vice-president of the Ramblers Association.

Roy Strong was Director of the Victoria and Albert Musuem. His many best-selling books include *Gardening through the Ages* and *The Story of Britain*.

Lisa Tickner has written widely on suffrage, including an influential account of the visual culture of suffrage campaigns, *The Spectacle of Women: Imagery of the Suffrage Campaign 1907–1914*.

Polly Toynbee is an outspoken journalist for *The Guardian*. She received the British Journalism Award for Columnist of the Year in 1998.

Carol Vorderman is a television presenter best known for work with mathematics and science programmes such as *Tomorrow's World*.

Kirsty Wark presents BBC2's Newsnight and has written *Building a Nation* (with Ranald MacInnes).

Marina Warner is a novelist and critic whose books cover subjects as diverse as fairy tales, popular culture, cinema, the Virgin Mary and Joan of Arc.

Gilda Williams is Commissioning Editor for Phaidon Press and an art writer.

Jane and Louise Wilson work together as video artists. They are currently working on the opening exhibition for the new Baltic gallery in Gateshead later this year.

Jacqueline Wilson is a journalist and award-winning children's author most recently publishing *Dustbin Baby*.

Acknowledgements

We would like to give our thanks to the following for making the exhibition 'Cooks and Campaigners' possible:

Judith Bourne
Howard & Constable
Mary Evans Picture Library
Peter Goodman
Anne Gray
Martyn Lello
Penny Martin
Roy Manderville
Kate Pullinger
Bob Venning
Pauline Webber
Ian Whybrow
Christine Wise
Wright & Wright

The Women's Library staff

Gill Barrow
Parhanaz Begum
Rebecca Bramell
Helen Bright
Catherine Burke
Gail Cameron
Hilary Clay
Liza Giffen
Jo Green
Jennifer Haynes
Sonia Hope
Victoria Killick
Catherine Norman
Ursulla O'Mahoney
Natalie Pollecutt
Richard Read
Amy Rowland
Dianne Shephard
Wendy Thomas
Maxine Willett
Roberta Wiseman

The Women's Library is a part of London Guildhall University and is supported by

The Arts and Humanities Research Board
Bridge House Estates Trust Fund
Calouste Gulbenkian Foundation
Cityside Regeneration
The Clore Duffield Foundation
The Clothworkers' Foundation
The Esmée Fairbairn Charitable Trust
The Heritage of London Trust
The Heritage Lottery Fund
Higher Education Funding Council of England
Joint Higher Education Funding Council
The London Development Agency
The Mercer's Company
The Paul Hamlyn Foundation
The Pilgrim Trust
The Rayne Foundation
Research Support Library Programme
South East Museums Services

The Friends of The Women's Library and many individual donors

LONDON GUILDHALL
UNIVERSITY